Hauntology

Katy Shaw

Hauntology

The Presence of the Past in Twenty-First Century
English Literature

palgrave
macmillan

Katy Shaw
Department of Humanities
Northumbria University
Newcastle Upon Tyne, UK

ISBN 978-3-319-74967-9   ISBN 978-3-319-74968-6   (eBook)
https://doi.org/10.1007/978-3-319-74968-6

Library of Congress Control Number: 2018937968

Cover illustration: © nemesis2207/Fotolia.co.uk

Printed on acid-free paper

This Palgrave Macmillan imprint is published by the registered company Springer International Publishing AG part of Springer Nature
The registered company address is: Gewerbestrasse 11, 6330 Cham, Switzerland

For Mark Fisher: A Scholar of the Future

ACKNOWLEDGEMENTS

This book would not have been possible without a great team of supporters. Biggest thanks to Ben Doyle at Palgrave Macmillan for his infinite positivity and to Camille Davies for getting the Pivot to print. A huge debt of gratitude is also extended to Professor Deborah Philips for offering critical readings of draft versions for the meagre price of gin and a mention in the acknowledgements. Done!

Special thanks for David Peace, and to Faber, for granting access to a manuscript copy of *Patient X* prior to its publication. David has extended his unswerving support and enthusiasm for this work since day one and for that, and his friendship, I am eternally grateful.

A sabbatical from Leeds Beckett University was instrumental to the writing process. Particular thanks for critical conversations go to some brilliant academic women: Dr Rachel Connor, Dr Caroline Herbert, Professor Susan Watkins and Professor Gina Wisker. Support from Northumbria University was vital in finishing the work and many thanks for this go to Professor Julian Wright, Professor Richard Terry and Dr Katherine Baxter.

Personal thanks, as always, to my parents for their unconditional love, and to my brother for reading draft versions of Chapter 3. Thanks also to my friends for putting up with the strange obsessions of academic life. Special thanks to Dan, for everything.

During the writing of this book, the world lost one of its leading hauntology scholars. Mark Fisher was a unique and original thinker whose influence haunts this work. His contribution to the field was defining, and his loss tragic. The following study was written with the intention of continuing the work of K-Punk into the future—informed by his writings, and inspired by his spirit.

CONTENTS

Introduction. Hauntology: Ghosts of Our Lives — 1

1 The (Spectral) Turn of the Century in Simon Armitage's 'Killing Time' (1999) — 25

2 Phantasmal Intertexts: Literary Spectrality in Jez Butterworth's *Jerusalem* (2009) — 43

3 'Ghostpitality': Specters of the Self in Zadie Smith's *NW* (2012) — 59

4 Authorial Afterlives: Ghost-writing in David Peace's *PATIENT X* (2018) — 83

Conclusion. 'In Return': Towards a Hauntology of Twenty-First Century English Literature — 105

Bibliography — 111

Index — 117

Introduction. Hauntology: Ghosts of Our Lives

Abstract Hauntology is a peculiarly English phenomenon. Karl Marx famously claimed that his Communist revolution would start in England and, more than a hundred years on, England has become a haunt for the specters of its most recent past. The existence of this Pivot is a timely reminder of the ever growing and changing field of critical and popular enquiry on hauntology. Hauntology destabilizes space as well as time, and encourages an 'existential orientation' in the haunted subject, making the living consider the precarious boundary between being and non-being. By the new millennium, hauntology had become part of the *zeitgeist* of academic and popular criticism in England. In areas as diverse as architecture and music, art and psychoanalysis, a range of critics harnessed Derrida's concept as a critical lens through which to read a twenty-first century English culture seemingly more concerned with co-opting the past than embracing the future.

Keywords Hauntology • Literature • Past • Present • Derrida • Haunt • Deconstruction • English • Contemporary

1

Hauntology is a peculiarly English phenomenon. Karl Marx famously claimed that his Communist revolution would start in England and, more than a hundred years on, England has become a haunt for the specters of its most recent past. The existence of this Pivot is a timely reminder of the ever growing and changing field of critical and popular enquiry on hauntology. Hauntology is 'a science of ghosts, a science of what returns'.[1] It destabilizes space as well as time, and encourages an 'existential orientation'[2] in the haunted subject, making the living consider the precarious boundary between being and non-being. While hauntology may be dismissed by some 'as merely one more French, fashionable and nonsensical term',[3] it is notable for capturing 'a zeitgeist, something which is already in place and which demands critical commentary (and extrapolative extension)'.[4] By the new millennium, hauntology had become part of the *zeitgeist* of academic and popular criticism in England. In areas as diverse as architecture and music, art and psychoanalysis, a range of critics harnessed Derrida's concept as a critical lens through which to read a twenty-first century English culture seemingly more concerned with co-opting the past than embracing the future.

The experience of being haunted is one of noticing absences in the present, recognizing fissures, gaps and points of crossover. Hauntology gestures toward the '*agency of the virtual*',[5] since the specter is not of the here-and-now, yet is capable of exercising a spectral causality over the living. In popular culture, the specter is often represented through a series of 'persistences, repetitions, prefigurations'[6] that speak both to and of that particular cultural moment. Rather than being lost in the act of reproduction (as Walter Benjamin's critique of mass produced art feared), the spectral return instead bestows a new purpose and agency that functions to replace the original. As Fredric Jameson acknowledges, hauntology encourages us to recognize that 'the living present is scarcely as self-sufficient as it claims to be; that we would do well not to count on its density and solidity, which might under exceptional circumstances betray us'.[7] In dissolving the separation between now and then, the specter points towards the dual directions of hauntology—the compulsion to repeat the past, and an anticipation of the future. Haunting its own ontology, hauntology draws attention to the ephemeral nature of the present and offers the specter as neither being or non-being, alive or dead—the ultimate conceptual, and cultural, paradox.

While 'every period has its ghosts',[8] and every culture is haunted differently, this book reflects a twenty-first century English view on the subject in its consideration of how and why contemporary English literature deploys spectrality to represent interconnections between the past, present and future. It argues that an obsession with the recent past has become a major informing influence on twenty-first century English literature, one that has led to a new range of hauntological writings that profile the spectral and its capacity as a critical tool for comprehending the post-millennial period. Examining representations of spectrality across poetry, drama, the novel and short story, the following chapters consider how and why the spectral is being used to represent the changing anxieties and hopes of the new millennium in twenty-first century English literature.

Post-millennial writings function a useful prism through which to consider contemporary English culture and its compulsion to revisit the immediate past. The critical practice of hauntology turns to the past in order to make sense of the present, to understand how we got to this place and how to build a better future. Since the year 2000, popular culture has been inundated with representations of those who occupy a space between being and non-being, who defy ontological criteria. Contemporary English literature represents a twenty-first century world that is full of specters, reminiscence and representations of spectral encounters. These specters become visible and significant as they interact with a range of social, political and economic discourses that continue to speak to the contemporary period. In contrast to nineteenth and twentieth century English literature, and its fascination with defining or capturing the specter, twenty-first century English literature is not only interested in how we have come to live with specters, but in how we are living with them, and the ways in which popular culture is tracing this process of 'living with'. This enduring fascination with the spectral offers valuable insights into a contemporary English culture in which spectral manifestations signal towards larger social anxieties, as well as to specific historical events and recurrent cultural preoccupations. The specter confronts the contemporary with the necessity of participation, encouraging the realization that we must engage with it in order to create meaning. Narrative agency is the primary motivating force of the return, since the repetition of the specter often functions to highlight new meanings and perspectives. As such, this Pivot is concerned with the conditions of visibility of specters—of where they appear and in what form, to whom they appear and which knowledges from the past they (re) present in the contemporary moment. Harnessing hauntology as a lens through which to consider the specters haunting twenty-first century English writings, the following chapters chronicle the emergence of a vein of hauntological literature that profiles the pervasive presence of the past across writings produced in the new millennium.

STAGING SPECTERS

By the time of his death in 2004, Derrida had become one of the greatest French philosophers of all time, the subject of two movies and several media scandals. Even for his many fans, Derrida was, and remains, a 'frustrating thinker'[9] whose work is characterized by complicated conundrums, deliberate verbosity and academic game-playing. As the inventor of 'deconstruction', Derrida shaped an entire generation of thinkers in the arts, humanities and social sciences. Deconstruction raises the specter of doubt as its central tenant: nothing is fixed, firm or stable in the hands of deconstructionists. Inherent in the deconstructive approach is the privileging of the logic of presence by the function of *différance*. Deconstructionists are concerned with moving concepts from the margins to the centre—as in the privileging of writing over speech, for example— in order to examine the creation of power and meaning. The importance of deconstruction lies in its central thesis that language is inherently unstable and its meaning indeterminable. Deconstructionists argue that language is always open to the wide-ranging analysis of interpretation and subjectivity, and that meaning and understanding are therefore always fluid and contextual. As Stuart Sim wryly notes, 'the difference between the Mafia and deconstruction is that the former makes you an offer you can't refuse, the latter an offer you can't understand'.[10]

The 1990s marked a shift in the explicit political consciousness of Derrida's work—most notably in his essay 'Force of Law'—when he began to consider deconstruction as a means of achieving justice.[11] His 1994 translated text *Specters of Marx: The State of the Debt, the Work of Mourning and the New International* offers a statement on the relationship between deconstruction and Marxism at the end of the twentieth century. While Derrida argued that *Specters of Marx* was not simply a project about 'deconstructive politics', he also acknowledged that the text marked a point at which he felt a responsibility to say something more about politics, to address the political capacity of Marx in the post-Soviet period, and to extend his spectral thinking in the pursuit of justice. Despite the fact that it is replete with references to death, quotations about 'passing' and a series of endings, *Specters of Marx* actually presents a case for change and reform, and offers new understandings of the spectral presence of the past in contemporary life.

In *Specters of Marx*, Derrida argues that the dominant narrative of the post-Cold War era was one of the death of an alternative to capitalism as a global system, and bemoans what he identifies as 'a dominant discourse, or rather one that is on the way to becoming dominant [...]. Marx is dead, communism is dead, very dead, and along with it its hopes, its discourse, its theories, and its practices. It says: long live capitalism, long live the market, here's to the survival of economic and political liberalism!'[12] In the late twentieth century, the Berlin Wall constituted an apparent binary divider between East and West, Capitalist and Communist, Right and Left. Its fall on 9 November 1989 was heralded by historian Francis Fukuyama as marking 'the end of history' and by hauntology scholar Mark Fisher as the dawn of 'capitalist realism: the widespread sense that not only is capitalism the only viable political and economic system, but also that it is now impossible even to *imagine* a coherent alternative to it'.[13] Yet, in Derrida's eyes, the fall of the Berlin Wall did not signal the 'end of history', but the destabilization of the formerly 'fixed' binaries it had come to represent.

While Derrida was not the only critic to speak out—Baudrillard and Lyotard also wrote about notions of 'endism' in the closing decades of the twentieth century—he did stand as a powerful dissenting voice against Fukuyama and the voices of post-liberalism.[14] Derrida's *Specters of Marx* not only articulates concerns about these changes but also offers important alternatives to liberal capitalism for the future. In the text, Derrida traces a 'geneology'[15] of specters in Marx's work to suggest that Marxism has always and will always haunt society, and, in doing so, argues that the fall of the Berlin Wall will not simply negate its presence. The inheritance of Marx is 'that which continues to put back on the drawing board the question of life, spirit, or the spectral, of life-death beyond the opposition between life and death'.[16] Drawing on contextual developments in postmodernism and a wider rejection of metanarratives, with a 'commitment to doubleness [and] to the juxtaposition and equal weighting of [...] seeming contraries',[17] hauntology emerges from *Specters of Marx* as a concept capable of presenting new ways of thinking about the past, present and future, rather than just the 'end' of history and of the twentieth century.

Derrida uses a variety of terms to denote the ghostly, including phantasm, ghost, specter/spectre, apparition and revenant. Across the following pages, readers will note that cultural critics also adopt different terms to represent the returned. This study quotes each accordingly, but adopts 'specter' for its own arguments, since the term enjoys a special meaning in Derrida's writings. Unlike 'ghost' or 'revenant', the term 'specter' 'speaks of the spectacle', it 'is first and foremost something visible. It is of the visible, but of the invisible visible, it is the visibility of a body which is not present in flesh and blood.'[18] Spectrality can be hard to conceptualize, since it operates in the between-spaces that separate recognized boundaries; in doing so, it effectively draws attention to the limitations of such ontological categories and the limits of standard perception. The past and the present co-habit in the specter, whose visibility highlights 'a heterodidactics between life and death'.[19] The past is always in the present through the form of haunting, yet the specter is also necessarily 'an entity out of place in time' and, 'as something from the past that emerges into the present, the phantom calls into question the linearity of history'.[20] *Specters of Marx* signals this multiple dimension of spectrality, suggesting that there is a plurality in the discussions of their 'multiplicity' and 'heterogeneity'.[21] The word 'spirits'[22] is also frequently used in the text to denote the quantity of specters and the impossibility of a singular haunt.

The disparate demands and nature of the specter means that it defies logic, and can often appear contradictory in both form and function. Derrida argues that 'everything begins by the apparition of a specter'[23] but also underlines that 'the specter is a paradoxical incorporation [...]. One does not know if it is living or if it is dead.'[24] Spectres do not respect physical and metaphorical boundaries: 'they pass through walls, these revenants. Day and night, they trick consciousness and skip generations.'[25] The specter evokes a 'non-contemporaneity with itself or the living present',[26] and constitutes a peculiar presence. The paradoxical state of the specter is a product of its in-between condition, 'both visible and invisible, both phenomenal and nonphenomenal: a trace that marks the present with its absence in advance'.[27] Specters demand a form of responsibility but, as 'unstable interstitial figures that problematize dichotomous thinking',[28] they often raise more questions than they answer. Because ontology is incapable of representing the state of specters (both living and dead), hauntology develops as a way of articulating both the presence and absence that defines the spectral. The specter represents 'the visibility of the invisible',[29] but also raises questions of time and chronology. The non-presence of the specter demands that we take its history into consideration, foregrounding time and the temporality of the return.

Temporal Disjunctures

Time is central to the concept of hauntology. Haunting looks back to the past and points forward to the future from the moment of the present. In doing so, it signals towards a legacy as well as to a promise of something to come, drawing attention to the structuring role of absence. The encounter with the specter marks the point at which multiple temporalities meet and cross. As such, the specter 'de-synchronizes, it recalls us to anachrony'.[30] These points of intersection highlight the spectrality of reality, since the return of the past opens not only a spatial dimension, but also a breach in temporality wherein the presence-absence relationship creates a two-fold reality. *Specters of Marx* pointedly opens with an epigraph from *Hamlet* dedicated to these temporal disjunctions: 'The time is out of joint'. This immediately establishes a key theme of the text—the breaking down of delineations between past, present and future time—as well as highlighting the necessary conditions for the successful act of return, or haunting.

Specters disturb the present with the possibility of alternative pasts and futures. In doing so they also defy time and space, and challenge any fixity of the temporal. This spectral effect is predicated upon the return—the act of coming back—that questions the temporal boundaries of that which has happened, and that which is yet to come. *Specters of Marx* keeps returning to the idea that everything is 'spectral' in the sense that 'everything [...] comes back to haunt everything, everything is in everything, this is, "the class of specters"'.[31] The paradox of the specter is then perhaps best understood in terms of time, of a repetitious compulsion to return. The distortion of linear time that is required for manifestation means that 'there may be no proper time'[32] for specters; they instead function to draw attention to the limitations of time, and the ever-present role of the past in both the structure of haunting and the future of society.

For Derrida, the breaking down and challenging of preconceived, temporal boundaries constitutes one of the defining characteristics of the specter. He argues that 'before knowing whether one can differentiate between the specter of the past and the specter of the future, of the past present and the future present, one must perhaps ask oneself whether the spectrality effect does not consist in undoing this opposition, or even this dialectic, between actual, effective presence and its other'.[33] For the specter to return, there must be 'some disjointing, disjunction, or disproportion'.[34]

'A spectral moment' is both 'furtive and untimely' since 'the apparition of the specter does not belong to that time, it does not give time'.[35] The specter facilitates an encounter with the past, in the hope that it will shape our understanding of the present, and of the future.

In Derrida's work, specters represent a deconstructive perspective on time itself. They question 'a general temporality made up of the successive linking of presents identical to themselves and contemporary with themselves'.[36] They challenge limits between states of living and death, past and present and, in doing so, question notions of historicism by disrupting the linear pathway of historical time. Like deconstruction, the specter rejects any solidification of the past, shattering notions of temporality by signalling the return of the past subject in the present moment. In their attacks on history, identity and ontology, both deconstruction and the specter 'fracture fixities of meaning and open up new understandings and possibilities'.[37] Both are founded on an accepted instability, both defy fixed form or meaning, and both operate in profound defiance of binary oppositions. The specter calls into question any opposition between past and present, instead suggesting that these two apparently exclusive states can never be neatly separated.

The return marks the beginning, rather than the end, of the spectral exchange. The ontology of the performance of the haunt is intimately tied to the here-and-now of the present and the necessary conditions of visibility through which the specter makes itself manifest. The significance of the specter lies in a recognition of this repetition, of a return that appears in changed contexts and times. The notion of the spectral haunt challenges history by disrupting established chronologies of past, present and future. It gives voice to the hard-to-hear, it represents the formerly unrepresentable, and makes visible that which was previously ignored. In this way, as Blanco and Peeren argue, 'all history and memory may indeed be spectral in some sense'[38] since both operate at the margins of space and time. The appearance of the specter, a thing from the past in the present moment, marks a burden of the past on the present, and opens up the present to the many possibilities of that which came before. Operating across temporal zones, the specter, as something 'always both *revenant* (invoking what was) and *arrivant* (announcing what will come)' encourages us to focus on 'the future and its possible interactions with the present and past'.[39]

In Ken McMullen's 1983 experimental film *Ghost Dance*, Derrida famously asserts that 'the future belongs to ghosts' and argues that hauntology as a concept is concerned with the breaking down of chronological perception. 'Think[ing] the ghost'[40] involves thinking beyond or around accepted temporal boundaries. In coming back, the specter repeats itself but in a new performance, a new time, and a new space. The questions it raises are caused by this repetition, since 'a *specter* is always a revenant. One cannot control its comings and goings because it *begins by coming back.*'[41] Disrupting time and space, the specter highlights what Laclau calls an 'anachronism essential to spectrality: the specter, interrupting all spectrality, desynchronizes time'.[42]

To conceive of the presence of the specter is to conceive of an oxymoron, since 'to haunt does not mean to be present, and it is necessary to introduce haunting into the very construction of the concept'.[43] This 'constitutive dislocation [...] inhabits all hauntology' since the 'contamination of presence by the specter' of the past in a 'weakened form of incarnation'[44] in the present highlights a disjuncture of time. This disjuncture is jarring, because the specter represents something past, spent and ended, yet its (re)appearance in the present gestures towards a series of new beginnings. In the act of haunting, it is not the vision of the specter but the specter as possibility that is most interesting. Hauntology offers the specter as a metaphorical trope through which to disrupt the certainty of temporality and to open up meanings. This opening up is only possible if recognition and responsibility are enacted: the haunted subject must extend hospitality and speak to the specter in order for illumination to occur.

SPEAK TO THE SPECTER

The first rule of hauntology does not focus on the specter at all, but rather underscores the responsibility of the haunted subject to welcome, and speak to, the specter. Derrida asserts that we must 'learn to live with ghosts, in the upkeep, the conversation, the company, or the companionship, in the commerce without commerce of ghosts. To live otherwise, and better. No, not better, but more justly. But *with them.*'[45] This instruction is founded upon a sense of obligation. In the words of Avery Gordon, we 'have to talk to [the specter] graciously [...] we have to learn how it speaks and offer it a hospitable reception we must'.[46] Haunting is presented as the social reality of this 'living with' specters and *Specters of Marx* can be read as an etiquette guide on 'how to hospitably and delicately talk to ghosts' which, as Gordon makes clear, 'we must'.[47]

Derrida takes this one stage further, and repeatedly outlines our responsibility to welcome the specter unconditionally. He encourages 'hospitality without reserve, welcoming salutation accorded in advance to the absolute surprise of the *arrivant* from whom or from which one will not ask anything in return'. This, Derrida writes, 'is the very place of spectrality'.[48] This ethical act of hospitality without reserve, to open oneself up to another being with acceptance and without warning is a significant demand. With such acceptance comes risk. Since 'the ghost cannot be [...] managed',[49] we cannot know how long it has been watching us, when it will appear, the manner in which it will manifest itself, or the information it has returned to communicate. The decision to welcome the specter is therefore a difficult one. Yet such unconditional welcome is key since, according to Gordon, 'reckoning with ghosts is not like deciding to read a book: you cannot simply choose the ghosts with which you are willing to engage'.[50] In confronting and accepting the specter, we grant it hospitable memory out of 'a concern for justice'.[51]

But offering hospitality to the specter is not enough—we must learn to speak to the specter, 'not only to live with specters [...] but also to engage the ghost, [...] cooperatively, as metaphor, as weapon, as salve, as a fundamental epistemology for living'.[52] Derrida is firm in his assertion that 'it is necessary to speak of the ghost, indeed to the ghost and with it'.[53] Representing, addressing and engaging in dialogue with the specter, the act of the haunt requires the obscene to be rendered visible, the space to be highlighted, and the conjuring to take place. In doing so, we permit the specter to see, to act, to communicate, to 'give the ghost a voice and the ability to see without being seen: the power of the dead to watch over and address the living, to hold us accountable to their memory'.[54] Conversation is central since 'this being-with specters would also be, not only but also, a politics of memory, of inheritance, and of generations'[55]— a communicative exchange. The act of opening ourselves to the specter must come without reassurance or promise, it should arrive without 'expectation' or even 'anticipation' but in the form of a 'commitment'[56] to which we must dedicate ourselves. Despite a lack of awareness of what the specter will bring, the unconditional opening of the present to the past is a risk worth taking according to Derrida since 'the dead [...] are the door keepers who while closing one side "give" way to the other'.[57] The unexpected return of the specter represents an ethical injunction, a new awareness of what is now, and what could be in the future. The future possibilities opened up by the specter therefore offer a reward through the process of communicative exchange.

Receiving the specter is not a passive act—the 'performativity' of the specter is not a signal to sit and watch but a call for responsibility. In any encounter with the specter, lines of communication are not linear, but profoundly dialogic. We not do merely 'receive' the specter; we must enter into an act of engagement with it. Derrida admits that 'it takes some effort to recognize the ghost and to reconstruct the world it conjures up',[58] but argues that this is an effort that we must be willing to make. The wants and needs of the specter are nothing without the living—they need us to engage and form a communicative encounter. Through this relationship, they need us to recognize, remember and accommodate them. As Avery Gordon reminds us, 'the ghost is nothing without you' since 'haunting makes its only social meaning in contact with the living time of the now'.[59] Although it is related to something past, the specter is always current, its motivations and intervention are aimed at the present moment, and aim to highlight the precarious nature of that moment.

The need to 'learn to live *with* ghosts'[60] is significant because 'this being-with specters [is] not only but also, a politics of memory, of inheritance, and of generations' past and future.[61] How societies generate and receive specters is important because 'the dead can often be more powerful than the living'.[62] The past cannot simply be buried or denied: the specter must be received as an 'Other' from the past in order to activate its spectral agency in the present, and for the future. The responsibility of the living to take note of the inheritance signalled by the specter, to learn to live with the specter in order to reframe society and the self through the act of the return, is presented as central to any notion of future potentialities.

SPECTRAL AGENCY

While *Specters of Marx* is ostensibly about endings—the end of history, the end of an alternative to capitalism in a Post-Soviet era, the end of the influence of Marx in the modern world—the text critically examines these various endings as opportunities for fresh starts and new potentialities. In this context, the specter generates agency and change in the present, for the future. Despite representing something of the past, 'the specter, contrary to what good sense leads us to believe, signals toward the future'.[63] James Bridle underscores this approach in his argument that the concept of hauntology 'deals with the problem of the future by going back to the past'.[64] The specter comes from the past to cast new perspectives on the future. It suggests that 'what seems to be out front, the future, comes back in advance: from the past, from the back'[65] and in doing so 'questions with regard to what will come in the future-to-come'.[66] As a result, 'one can never distinguish between the future-to-come and the coming-back of a specter',[67] between a real or deferred present time, since the specter does not comply with the temporal linearity that structures our understanding of past, present and future in the contemporary world.

Founded on temporal disjuncture, the appearance of the specter suggests that 'the future [...] is not at one with the present'[68] and the specter itself represents an alternative that is 'energetically and future-orientated and active'.[69] For Frederic Jameson, the true potentiality of hauntology lies in this focus on the capacity of the spectral 'to open up wholly new and unexpected lines of rereading'.[70] He reflects that 'the appearance of the ghost [...] calls, to be sure, for a revision of the past, for the setting in place of a new narrative [...] but it does so by way of a thoroughgoing reinvention of our sense of the past altogether'.[71] The specter functions to highlight what has gone before us, to remind us of our responsibility to live consciously of this, and to use this knowledge to inform the future. Specters of the past are capable of communicating in the present about the future and, in doing so, launch the possibility of a different future to come. Yet, the 'specter of the past can only appear when conjured by the promise of another future'.[72] As Weinstock points out, since 'ghosts do "cultural work"',[73] the cultural task of the specter is to shed light on 'the extent to which the past governs our present and opens or forecloses possibilities for the future'.[74] An openess to alternative potentialities must exist in order for the apparition and exchange to take place, and for the question to be asked: what does the specter mean for the future?

Specters are profoundly social—they function to highlight future potentialities and, in turn, demand actions and decisions from the living. The appearance of the specter can therefore be understood as a call to social action. For Avery Gordon, as for Derrida, haunting 'is distinctive for producing a something-to-be-done'.[75] In her study on haunting in the sociological imagination, Gordon repeatedly asserts that 'haunting is part of our social world and understanding it is essential to grasping the nature of our society, and for changing it'.[76] Presenting the dead as social figures, and exploring their social effects, Gordon examines the capacity of the haunt as a means of understanding 'modern forms of dispossession, exploitation, repression, and their concrete impacts on the people most affected by them and on our shared conditions of living'.[77] Gordon argues that specters are analytical tools, metaphors with a powerful utility, and a means of empowerment for the present. She argues that 'the force of the ghost's desire is not just negative [...] [it is] pregnant with unfulfilled possibility, with the something to be done that the wavering present is demanding. This something to be done is not the return of the past.'[78] Its appearance in the present presents new knowledge and a new form of resistance to received narratives of the past, and sets 'in place a different future'. [79]

Significantly, Gordon warms that we ignore the dead at our peril, since 'the dead shape the lives we are able to live'.[80] In accepting the need to live with specters, we are also reminded of the ethical injunction not to forget, since 'the ghost remains that which gives one the most to think about—and to do'.[81] The active tense of this claim is important since it foregrounds the encounter as one of dual agency—it is our duty to note how and why specters rupture the present and our ethical responsibility to listen to and live with them. The act of the haunt represents 'that moment in which we recognize [...] that it could have been and can be otherwise'.[82] The specter returns from the past to make us act in the present, it presents us with a possibility, an acknowledgement of the past and a re-imagining of the future. In its tripartite haunting, the specter resists any finite end to the past, and instead encourages a new awareness of the role of the past in the present of contemporary culture.

NOW/THEN/NOW/THEN

For many cultural and political commentators in England, the beginning of the twenty-first century was characterized by dislocation, and dissatisfaction. Legal legacies of the previous decade continued to haunt contemporary English society in the form of investigations into Operation Yewtree and the legacy of TV presenter child abuse scandals, justice appeals for victims of Hillsborough and Orgreave, reports into the Iraq War and the Leveson Enquiry into phone hacking and news media bias. Culturally, odes to 1970s and 1980s culture dominated television, film, music, and fashion while, politically, the death of former Prime Minister Margaret Thatcher drew attention to the unresolved conflicts of these decades still active in English society. This sense of haunting gave rise to a twenty-first century England obsessed by its 'culture full of ghosts'.[83] As Mark Fisher notes: 'By the end of 2012, the 70s was returning, no longer as some bittersweet nostalgia trip, but as a trauma.'[84] Retro-culture created an uncomfortable paradox between a sense of cultural proximity to the period, and a socio-political desire to demonstrate distance from its mis-uses of power. Harnessed to conjure a past that never was, the popular culture of the past fifty years returned to haunt the post-millennial English subject.

As critical vehicles capable of disrupting the narrative present, spectral visitations can perhaps be best understood as responses to our own cul-tural moment and the anxieties pertinent to our age. Slavoj Žižek claims that the return of the dead is 'the fundamental fantasy of contemporary mass culture',[85] and in many ways contemporary popular culture itself can be viewed as a form of 'ghostly space [...] it remains an elusive, contested concept with blurry boundaries'.[86] According to Blanco and Peeren, as context-specific entities, 'each age has its own ghosts'[87] and these 'ghosts [...] appear at specific moments, and specific locations'.[88] The fact that 'ghosts are particularly prominent in our cultural moment indicates that we are particularly vexed by these questions. The ghosts that we conjure speak to these timely, context-bound fears and desires—they can do noth-ing else.'[89]

One of the most significant threats to the cultural production of the future is the presiding presence of the past. Nietzsche argues that an age can become oversaturated with the past, to the point whereby a cultural stultifying takes place. He argues that 'oversaturation of an age with his-tory' can lead to that period having a 'dangerous mood of irony in regard to itself and subsequently into the even more dangerous mood of cyni-cism'.[90] In his critical study on the role of retro in contemporary culture, Simon Reynolds argues that 'Instead of being about itself, the 2000s has been about every other previous decade happening again all at once [...]. Instead of being the threshold to the future, the first ten years of the twenty-first century turned out to be the "Re" Decade. The 2000s were dominated by the "re-" prefix: *re*vivals, *re*issues, *re*makes, *re*-enactments. Endless *re*trospection.'[91] Haunted by the sense that it could not articulate the present, contemporary English culture became marked by a sense of failed mourning, a refusal to give up a past that it had not yet resolved.

The cultural context of the new century did not then evidence a hun-ger for the 'new' in English culture as much as it did an appetite for the revivification of cultural representations of and from the past fifty years, in both mainstream and alternative culture and across a variety of cultural forms. For Fisher, this near-constant 'temporal bleed-through from ear-lier periods' created a sense that 'the twenty first century is oppressed by a crushing sense of finitude and exhaustion. It doesn't feel like the future.'[92] Instead of being a productive generator of new representations, contemporary English culture of the new millennium seemed to be 'rife with retro', leading critics to worriedly hypothesize 'what happens when we run out of past?'[93] As a decade of revival rather than futurism, 2000–2010 created concern among cultural critics that greater focus should be placed on the moment of cultural production, that the retrospection of the new century was leading to an obsession with the specters of the past as opposed to the potentiality of the future. As a result, cultural critics began to worry that English culture was trapped in a kind of counter-productive limbo, spectralized into paralysis by the overwhelming presence of the immediate past. For a culture stuck at the 'end of history', hauntology offered not only a marker of the times, but a way of articulating the inertia and anachronism of the contemporary in critical ways.

Ghost Writing

Literature enjoys its own internal hauntology, both in the multi-faceted capacity of language to carry a multitude of meanings, the power of intertextuality to communicate from beyond the confines of the immediate text and in the power of literary testimony to communicate unheard voices and unspoken perspectives. Derrida confessed to having a 'taste (probably unconditional) for literature, more precisely for literary writing'[94] precisely because of its capacity to demonstrate this multi-layered potentiality of meaning that is characteristic of his own deconstruction. In his short text 'Literature in Secret', he explores the 'spectral quality of literature' and the implication that 'its being a specter—means that it is not an existent or being nor a localizable remains or archive but belongs to a future [...]. As a specter, literature is neither spirit nor body and both at the same time, which makes it difficult to name.' Since there is 'no essence of literature, no truth of literature, no literary-being or being-literary of literature'[95] it constitutes a spectral form.

In his assertion that 'the specters are textual',[96] Mark Fisher alludes to Derrida's speculation that texts can be considered as inherently spectral, that 'literature has always been the uncanny site par excellence'.[97] Through a series of passing references to the 'spectral dynamic of literature',[98] Derrida highlights that the ontology of literature is not fixed, but rather occupies a state that is in-between, oscillating and open to interpretation. Since 'writing, textuality [...] and haunting are not only interrelated; they are inseparable',[99] hauntology problematizes the notion of textuality itself. The reciprocal nature of the intertextual haunt functions to create dissonance rather than harmony, throwing new light on the original writing as well as its unresolved connections to later texts. It requires an established horizon of expectation in the reader and a recognized awareness of the original writing and its concerns, in order for the meaning of its spectral presence in the later text to be acknowledged, and understood. This relationship profiles the literary form as necessarily intertextual and haunted, a site of potential spectral agency.

In his reflection that 'I think one writes also *for* the dead',[100] Derrida posits the act of literary representation as a political one that bestows agency and dynamism in the present. The indeterminable ontology of literature means that is an appropriate site to open up ideas about possibility and to challenge boundaries of time and space. Hauntology then becomes 'part of an endeavour to keep raising the stakes of literary study, to make it a place where we can interrogate our relation to the dead, examine the elusive identities of the living, and explore the boundaries between the thought and the unthought'.[101] The literary act or encounter is inextricably haunted since the spectral lies at the heart of narrative. The act of consuming a text in the present gives the past a voice, and often many conflicting narrative voices which the reader must pick through, negotiate with and judge. Hauntology and spectrality thereby offer a useful conceptual framework for reading as a literary portal through which the specter can make itself manifest. Since the year 2000, a range of new English literary texts have sought to explore aspects of hauntological praxis by raising concepts of nostalgia and memory, mobilizing sample-like intertextuality and representing the agency of the return. While the following discussion offers a range of examples in terms of form and style, it is necessarily subject to the brevity of the Pivot form, and is conditioned by the evolving conceptions of hauntology present in contemporary cultural criticism at the time of writing. As such, this Pivot does not claim to be exhaustive, but rather offers an exploratory introduction to a range of contemporary English literary specters—their appearances, habitats, behaviours and manifestations—in a taxonomical approach.

The spectral trope functions as a popular method of representing the return across twenty-first century writings, whether in the form of a symbol that is repeated, a refrain that appears frequently in dialogue or narrative, or an item, word, or sound that punctuates the text at regular points. The following chapters offer explorations of haunting and considerations of the notion of the return, across historical, social and cultural contexts as part of a wide project to understand representations of the role of the past in the present in twenty-first century English Literature. Chapter 1 explores the function of the spectral trope as an unexpected repetition from the past designed to create new meaning in the present. In Simon Armitage's long poem 'Killing Time' (1999), a range of social and cultural tropes associated with the liminal, the historical and the uncanny combine to bring the most recent past into a new focus. Highlighting the contested space and time of the historical record, and of the literary, the chapter explores how and why emergent structures of feeling haunt Armitage's ostensibly celebratory poem with spectral traces of its most recent history, casting long shadows over humanity's perceived lack of progress in the millennial moment.

Writing shares a spectral inclination towards openness, plurality and instability, Buse and Scott reflect that 'literature has always been a more accommodating place for ghosts, perhaps because fiction itself shares their simulacral qualities: like writing, ghosts are associated with a certain secondariness or belatedness'.[102] As amalgamations of other writers' materials, texts enjoy an intertextual dynamic with a network of exterior texts, alluding, connecting to or recycling narratives and characters, symbols and motifs. Through his dramatic explorations of the hauntological nature of intertextuality, English playwright Jez Butterworth problematizes the notion of rewriting and the relationship of new works to source texts. In his contemporary dramas, this takes the form of the appropriation of ancient stories and forms to articulate present experience, the haunting possession of previous works and the haunting mobilization of additional representations and narratives from social, political or economic spheres. Conceptualizing the relations of the return through a sense of referential relation or an uncannily haunting expression of unsettlement, Chapter 2 considers this use of phantasmal intertextuality as a form of spectral agency to examine 'ways in which plays and performance can be newly analysed and understood through a focus on tropes of the ghostly and representations of haunting'.[103] In considering how and why intertextual subjects emerge again in Butterworth's most famous stage drama, it surveys extensive meta-textual connectivities to examine the function of intertextual haunts on the contemporary English stage. Exploring the haunting use of intertextuality in Butterworth's *Jerusalem* (2009),[104] the chapter considers how and why this play ingests exterior texts in its narrative of the present, and demands reconsideration of the role of the past in the present.

Specters of Marx speaks to a series of spectro-geographic concerns: the geography of ghosts, the role of spectral landscapes, and the space, as well as the time, of the specter. Critics have noted the 'uncanny spiritual topography of Derrida's work',[105] his focus on a series of sites and spaces through which to frame the logics of haunting and the spectral and the intersection of time and space than enables the spectral visitation. Chapter 3 considers how the agency of the past in the present can produce new narratives generated from new temporal and spatial intersections and that operate across conventional borders of phenomenology and ontology. Through spatial metaphors or representations in texts, the haunted site can function as an enabling location through which 'reading the past lives of places [...] offer us lessons in how to explain them to the future'.[106] The etymology of the word 'haunt' also carries spatial connotations, through reference to a home, or the journey back to an original dwelling place. In Derrida's theory of the spectral, the home is not a safe site, but rather exists as a borderland in which liminal states exist side by side. In Zadie Smith's novel *NW* (2012),[107] spectral dimensions of the homely and the domestic link the 'haunt' to the compulsion to return to a place, as well as to notions of unconditional hospitality to the spectral 'Other'. In their connections with the architecture and geography of Smith's North West London, the specters of her novel critically frame England's capital city as a spectral site through a series of problematic encounters with the consequences of offering unconditional hospitality to the specter. Beginning with a titular concern with space and place, *NW* goes on to establish an extensive exploration of spectral topographies that are mobilized by its various narratives to represent the intrusion of the past in the present of contemporary England.

As a form of repetitive double, the specter is activated when the haunted subject engages in dialogue and narrates it into being. Chapter 4 considers how the capacity of the specter as a double suggests unresolved terms in David Peace's *romanzo di raconti*—a novel of tales, or 'short story cycle'—*Patient X* (2018).[108] Throughout this text, doubling is etymologically connected to the spectral and the ways in which the uncanniness of the specter can alert the living to its pervading presence in their own contemporary world. The dynamic of this relationship forms a central concern of Peace's short story cycle. In each tale, spectral effects impact on notions of the self, challenging the singular 'I' and raising the possibility of an/other. Through a subtle noise, movement, interactive vision or tactile encounter, the textual presentation of the specter generates questions regarding identity and existentialism. Across twelve short stories, the spectral takes various significant forms, functioning to highlight the unexpected nature of the return, and to raise questions about the self and the Other, the individual and society, and our understandings of historical situatedness.

Hauntology is motivated by an interest in illuminating a past we do not know, as well as preventing us from forgetting a history we would sometimes rather not know. The conclusion draws together the readings offered by the previous four chapters to examine how and why hauntological representations in contemporary English Literature can function to highlight unresolved connections to the recent past. The representation of the haunt as repeated time in twenty-first century English literature demonstrates that the past cannot and will not be 'fixed'. The traumas and narratives it illuminates are so profound that they encourage the reimagining of time and space, a submission to a chrono-consciousness of the displaced and invaded. Through hauntology we are encouraged to see the contemporary world as one of absence and disappearance, but also one of remembrance. The past daunts the contemporary that desires to excise its presence, but cannot. In a phantomic reality full of specters, this Pivot argues that hauntology encourages a reading of the post-millennial as a profoundly haunted period, one that seeks to defamiliarize our most recent past and demands that we re-evaluate its relevance in the present, and for the future.

NOTES

1. Pierre Macherey, 'Marx Dematerialised, or the Spirit of Derrida', Michael Sprinker (ed.) *Ghostly Demarcations: A Symposium on Jacques Derrida's Specters of Marx* (London: Verso, 2008) p. 18.
2. Mark Fisher, *Ghosts of My Life* (Winchester: Zero Books, 2014) p. 21.
3. Elisabeth M. Loevlie, 'Faith in the Ghosts of Literature. Poetic Hauntology in Derrida, Blanchot and Morrison's Beloved', *Religions*, 2013, 4, pp. 336–350; p. 337.
4. Mark Fisher, 'SPECTERS OF ACCELERATIONISM', *K-Punk: Abstract Dynamics*, 28 October 2008 <http://k-punk.abstractdynamics.org/archives/010782.html>
5. Fisher, 2014, p. 18.
6. Fisher, 2014, p. 28.
7. Frederic Jameson, 'Marx's Purloined Letter', Michael Sprinker (ed.), *Ghostly Demarcations: A Symposium on Jacques Derrida's Specters of Marx* (London: Verso, 2008) p. 39.

8. Jacques Derrida, *Specters of Marx: The State of the Debt, the Work of Mourning and the New International* (trans.) Peggy Kamuf (London: Routledge, 1994) p. 193.
9. Fisher, 2014, p. 16.
10. Stuart Sim, *Postmodern Encounters: Derrida and the End of History* (Cambridge: Icon Books UK, 1999) p. 10.
11. Jacques Derrida, 'Force of Law: The "Mystical Foundation of Authority"', in: *Deconstruction and the Possibility of Justice*, Drucilla Cornell, Michel Rosenfeld and David Gray Carlson (eds.) (London: Routledge, 1992) pp. 3–67.
12. Derrida teases out the spectral elements of Marx's work, his 'spectropoetic' obsession with specters and spirits, and extends it into a concept of hauntology that works to open up the present to the past, and future. Derrida notes that the noun 'specter' appears three times on the first page of *The Communist Manifesto*, which opens with the infamous statement that 'A specter is haunting Europe—the specter of communism' (Derrida, 1994, p. 20). This dual focus on spectrality and on Marx, is mobilized to segue into a wider discussion of the specters that haunt both Marx's writing and the spirit of Marxism that now haunts the contemporary world (Derrida, 1994, p. 64).
13. Mark Fisher, *Capitalist Realism* (Winchester: Zero Books, 2009) p. 2.
14. See also Jean Baudrillard, *The Illusion of the End* (trans.) Chris Turner (Stanford: Stanford University Press, 1994); Jean-Francois Lyotard, *Postmodern Condition: A Report on Knowledge (Theory & History of Literature)* (Manchester: Manchester University Press, 1984).
15. Derrida, 1994, p. 107.
16. Derrida, 1994, p. 54.
17. Jospeh Natoli and Linda Hutcheon (eds.) *A Postmodern Reader* (New York: State University Press of New York, 1993) p. xi.
18. Derrida quoted in Maria del Pilar Blanco and Esther Peeren (eds.) *The Spectralities Reader* (London: Bloomsbury, 2013) p. 38.
19. Derrida, 1994, p. xviii.
20. Jeffrey Andrew Weinstock, 'Introduction to The Spectral Turn', in Maria del Pilar Blanco and Esther Peeren, *The Spectralities Reader* (London: Bloomsbury, 2013) p. 62.
21. Derrida, 1994, p. 2.
22. Derrida, 1994, p. xx.
23. Derrida, 1994, p. 203.
24. Derrida, 1994, p. 5.
25. Derrida, 1994, p. 36.
26. Derrida, 1994, p. xix.
27. Blanco and Peeren, 2013, p. 39.

28. Weinstock in Blanco and Peeren, 2013, p. 62.
29. Derrida, 1994, p. 125.
30. Derrida, 1994, p. 7.
31. Derrida, 1994, p. 108.
32. P. Buse and A. Stott (eds.) *Ghosts: Deconstruction, Psychoanalysis, History* (London: Palgrave, 1999) p. 1.
33. Derrida, 1994, p. 48.
34. Derrida, 1994, p. xix.
35. Derrida, 1994, p. xix.
36. Derrida, 1994, p. 70.
37. Buse and Stott, 1999, p. 2.
38. Blanco and Peeren, 2013, p. 15.
39. Blanco and Peeren, 2013, p. 13.
40. Derrida, 1994, p. 25.
41. Derrida, 1994, p. 11.
42. Ernesto Laclau, 'The Time Is out of Joint', *Diacritics*, Vol. 25, No. 2 (Summer 1995) pp. 85–96; p. 87.
43. Derrida, 1994, p. 161.
44. Laclau, 1995, p. 86–88.
45. Derrida, 1994, pp. xvii–xviii.
46. Avery Gordon, *Ghostly Matters: Haunting and the Sociological Imagination* (Minneapolis: University of Minnesota Press, 2008) p. 208.
47. Gordon, 2008, p. 182.
48. Derrida, 1994, p. 65.
49. Gordon, 2008, p. 127.
50. Gordon, 2008, p. 190.
51. Derrida, 1994, p. 220.
52. Gordon, 2008, p. 151.
53. Derrida, 1994, p. xviiii.
54. Timothy Raphael, 'Mo(u)rning in America: Hamlet, Reagan, and the Rights of Memory', *Theatre Journal*, Vol. 59, No. 1 (March 2007) pp. 1–20; p. 20.
55. Derrida, 1994, p. viii.
56. Jacques Derrida, *Memories: For Paul de Man* (New York: Columbia University Press, 1986) p. 47.
57. Hélène Cixous, *Three Steps on the Ladder of Writing* (New York: Columbia University Press, 1994) p. 5.
58. Derrida quoted in Gordon, 2008, p. 66.
59. Gordon, 2008, p. 179.
60. Derrida, 1994, p. xvii.
61. Derrida, 1994, p. xix.
62. Derrida, 1994, p. 48.

63. Derrida, 1994, p. 196.
64. James Bridle, 'Hauntological Futures', *booktwo.org*, 20 March 2011 <http://booktwo.org/notebook/hauntological-futures/>
65. Derrida 1994, p. 10.
66. Derrida, 1994, p. xix.
67. Derrida, 1994, p. 46.
68. Jameson in Sprinker, 2008, p. 59.
69. Jameson in Sprinker, 2008, p. 60.
70. Jameson in Sprinker, 2008, p. 44.
71. Jameson in Sprinker, 2008, p. 43.
72. Werner Hamacher quoted in in Frederic Jameson, 'Marx's Purloined Letter', Michael Sprinker (ed.) *Ghostly Demarcations: A Symposium on Jacques Derrida's Specters of Marx* (London: Verso, 2008) p. 197.
73. Weinstock in Blanco and Peeren, 2013, p. 65.
74. Weinstock in Blanco and Peeren, 2013, p. 66.
75. Gordon, 2008, p. xvi.
76. Gordon, 2008, p. 27.
77. Gordon, 2008, p. xv.
78. Gordon, 2008, p. 183.
79. Gordon, 2008, p. 66.
80. Esther Schor, *Bearing the Dead: The British Culture of Mourning from the Enlightenment to Victoria* (London: Princeton University Press, 1994) p. 4.
81. Derrida, 1994, p. 122.
82. Gordon, 2008, p. 57.
83. Alex Murray, 'Hauntology; Or, Capitalism is Dead, Let's Eat it's Corpse!', MA Thesis, Manchester Metropolitan University, 2015.
84. Fisher, 2014, p. 89.
85. Slavoj Žižek, *Looking Awry: An Introduction to Jacques Lacan through Popular Culture* (London: The MIT Press, 1992) p. 22.
86. Slavoj Žižek quoted in Maria del Pilar Blanco and Esther Peeren (eds.), 'Introduction', *Popular Ghosts: The Haunted Spaces of Everyday Culture* (London: Continuum, 2010) p. xii
87. Blanco and Peeren, 2010, p. xi.
88. Blanco and Peeren, 2010, p. xi.
89. Weinstock in Blanco and Peeren, 2013, p. 64.
90. Friedrich Nietzsche, 'On the Uses and Disadvantages of History for Life' in Jeffrey K. Olick, Vered Vinitzky and Daniel Levy (eds.) *The Collective Memory Reader* (Oxford: Oxford University Press, 2011) pp. 73–79; p. 78.
91. Simon Reynolds, *Retromania: Pop Culture's Addiction to its Own Past* (London: Faber, 2012) p. xi.

92. Fisher, 2014, p. 5; p. 8.
93. Reynolds, 2012, p. xiv.
94. Jacques Derrida, *On the Name* Thomas Dutoit (ed.) (Stanford: Stanford University Press, 1995) p. 2.
95. Jacques Derrida, *The Gift of Death & Literature in Secret (Religion and Postmodernism)* (Chicago: Chicago University Press, 2008) p. 223.
96. Mark Fisher, 'Phonograph Blues', *K-Punk: Abstract Dynamics*, 19 October 2006 <http://k-punk.abstractdynamics.org/archives/008535.html>
97. Jacques Derrida quoted in Buse and Stott, 1999, p. 9.
98. Derrida quoted in Loevlie, 2013, p. 336.
99. Jodey Castricano, *Cryptomimesis: The Gothic and Jacques Derrida's Ghost Writing* (London: McGill-Queens University Press, 2001) p. 29.
100. Jacques Derrida, *The Ear of the Other: Otobiography, Transference, Translation: Texts and Discussions with Jacques Derrida* (trans.) Peggy Kamuf (Nebraska: University of Nebraska Press, 1988) p. 53.
101. Colin David, 'Etat Present: Hauntology, Specters and Phantoms' in Blanco and Peeren, 2013, p. 58.
102. Buse and Stott, 1992, p. 8.
103. Mary Luckhurst and Emilie Morin (eds.) *Theatre and Ghosts: Materiality, Performance and Modernity* (London: Palgrave, 2014) p. 5.
104. Jez Butterworth, *Jerusalem* (London: Nick Hern Books, 2009).
105. Castricano, 2001, p. 13.
106. Blanco and Peeren, 2013, p. 399.
107. Zadie Smith, *NW* (London: Penguin, 2012).
108. David Peace, *Patient X* (London: Faber, 2018).

CHAPTER 1

The (Spectral) Turn of the Century in Simon Armitage's 'Killing Time' (1999)

Abstract In Simon Armitage's long poem 'Killing Time' (1999), a range of social and cultural tropes associated with the liminal, the historical and the uncanny combine to bring recent events into a new focus. Highlighting the contested space and time of historical record, and of the literary, the chapter explores how and why emergent structures of feeling haunt Armitage's ostensibly celebratory poem, casting long shadows over humanity's perceived lack of progress in the millennial moment.

Keywords Time • Poetry • Past • Simon Armitage • Media • Millennial • Contemporary • Future • Haunting • Society • Contemporary

In his ambitious and controversial millennial poem 'Killing Time' (1999), English poet Simon Armitage scrutinizes a range of infamous events contemporaneous to the year 2000.[1] Considering the mediation of these era-defining incidents by the news media, and symbolic resonances with the state of humanity and civilization at the end of a thousand years, his text responds to widespread millennial anxieties by offering the poetic as a fitting form to engage with a range of concerns prescient to the period. Capturing the structures of feeling emergent in contemporary English society at the turn of the millennium, Armitage considers the ways in which literature can represent larger social processes and shifts in social practices. His long poem is haunted by an ontological dualism in which the past regularly intrudes on

© The Author(s) 2018
K. Shaw, *Hauntology*,
https://doi.org/10.1007/978-3-319-74968-6_2

the present. Reflecting the complex relations of these competing configurations, each section focuses on a social practice or process in-formation as the year 2000 approaches. From environmentalism and twenty-four hour news, to violent conflict, commercialization and the duality of time and memory, Armitage explores a network of emergent structures of feeling that cast a long shadow over the millennial moment.

'Killing Time' sutures the past, present and future, transporting residual inheritances from the previous millennium into a present moment of anxiety and expectation. Countering the hegemonic promotion of millennial celebrations, the poem illuminates the dynamics of new structures of feeling that offer alternative approaches to this iconic period. In between the gaps of mediated images and official representations of the millennial year, Armitage injects alternative experiences and discourses and appropriates these in the poetic form. Capturing a series of feelings in formation at the turn of the century, the emergent trajectory of his poem considers traces of embryonic tensions that come to characterize an iconic historic conjuncture. Disrupting popular understandings of history as a linear record that charts a perceived sense of progression, 'Killing Time' instead represents a millennial England trapped by the historical forces of its past, forces that persistently re-emerge in the present to challenge the foundations of contemporary identity and culture.

Y2K

Humanity is characterized by its perennial concern for the future, yet the fears and hysteria surrounding the coming of the year 1000 were nothing compared to those surrounding the advent of the year 2000.[2] For a generation that conceived of the future as a fascinating but frightening era, the impending start of the twenty-first century inspired growing alarm. A crowd psychology of speculation produced widespread concerns about a Y2K bug in technology, environmental and ecological disasters, and religious end-of-the-world prophecies. While it may appear 'astonishing that a mere date should work its way through a culture in so many different ways',[3] the volatility of this particular calendrical date inspired forms of deep psychological dread, and became a popular preoccupation. As Strozier argued in 1997, 'if once it took an act of imagination to think about the end of time, now it takes an act of imagination, or numbing, not to think about it'.[4] With its promise of both an ending and a re-birth, the year 2000 offered a prophetic quality of dualism, one that was as suggestive of potential pathways forwards, as it was of a collective demise.

Historically, the change of a millennia has always motivated a variety of creative responses and the late twentieth century was no exception. In literature, a new theme of collective endings and a marked growth in apocalyptic genres came to prominence as the new millennium approached. Frank Kermode attributes this trend to emergent feelings of 'eternal endism' during the 1990s, a centurial mysticism of fear rooted in human experience.[5] Novelist Don DeLillo argues that we should understand these late twentieth century creative works as expressions of a 'millennial hysteria',[6] artistic responses to a state of transition that led humanity to construct a series of cultural endings as frameworks through which to understand and elevate experience. In his own allegorical representation of the state of England at the turn of the millennium, Simon Armitage represents a culture haunted by the ghosts of its problematic past. Unable to confront the uncertainties of its present and threats of its future, in 'Killing Time', English society reluctantly moves towards a final countdown, and focal point of trauma, in the form of New Year's Eve, 1999.

To mark the occasion of the year 2000 in England, the New Millennial Experience Company (NMEC) was funded by the British government to commission the construction of a set of new architectural landmarks, including the Millennium Dome and Millennium Wheel in London, and the Millennium Stadium in Cardiff, Wales.[7] Alongside these permanent monuments to the millennium, the NMEC also commissioned a series of creative responses to the occassion from artists, writers and performers. Having lost out to Andrew Motion for the position of 'Poet Laureate' in early 1999,[8] Simon Armitage was named 'poet of the millennium'[9] later the same year. Following this accolade, the Poetry Society appointed Armitage as their poet in residence with the NMEC and commissioned him to write a new poem commemorating the year 2000. 'Killing Time' is the result of that commission.[10]

The millennium brief was part of the 1999 'Poetry Places' scheme that funded poets in residence in a diverse range of locations from supermarkets, to law firms and zoos, across England. As 'Millennial Poet', Armitage visited the twelve regions covered by the NMEC to see how the scheme was encouraging people to use poetry to understand their millennial context. He recalls that

> my residency was seeing how people had interpreted the occasion and used the money. NMEC may have thought I would put some of that into the poem, but I didn't, not directly. I was talking about larger issues. I think

they thought I was going to write about Ferris wheels, which I did, but maybe not in the way they expected.[11]

Armitage views 'Killing Time' as a form of 'public art' and recalls that in writing the poem 'what was liberating was not having to mind my p's and q's. I could mouth off.'[12] Asked about the pressure he felt to make a statement in his role as 'poet of the millennium', Armitage reflects that

> At the time I felt a certain amount of responsibility, and I knew people would be looking at 'Killing Time' and draw conclusions from it. But then I tend to do what I always do—retreat in to my head and then, in the end, it is between you and the page. I tried to write a poem on the modern media and the way our appetite for news is self-serving, which I felt was important. I think someone at *The Times* said I had written "a poison pen letter for the age", which I wanted to put on the back of the book. At the time I think they were expecting something soft and fluffy that rhymed, not expecting that piece I produced, which had its roots in Louis MacNeice's *Autumn Journal*. Perhaps that was not what people were looking for—not even the people who commissioned it.[13]

As a provocative response to the NMEC brief, 'Killing Time' underlines the public role of poetry as a form of moral and social intervention at the end of the twentieth century. Speaking in 1999, Armitage stated that he still believed there existed

> an appetite for poetry; there are times in our national consciousness where a poem feels like the right form of address. It is complicated—too much poetry, which is dense and obscure, in front of a non-specialist audience can be a disaster. I count myself lucky for living in a country that still has this person "the common reader"—if they see a poem in a magazine or a newspaper or one comes on the radio, they will stop and listen to it and have a reaction. We haven't arrived at the point where poetry is so obscure that it only exists in small dark corners.[14]

As a form of public poetry that actively attempts to engage with, rather than withdraw from, the social, economic and political issues active in its millennial moment, 'Killing Time' is written with a parodic awareness of all the historic events and literary texts that precede it. Through a combination of poetic retrospection, scathing satire, and ironic elegy—the first section offers a parody of Grey's earlier 'Elegy in a Country Churchyard' (1751)—Armitage offers poetry as a form of protest. Haunted by the content, style and epigraph of Grey's original work, 'Killing Time' is concerned with giving shape to personal and social experience and relating this to a sense of time past. Like Grey, Armitage uses his poem to recover the people and events that define a nation and a period, foregrounding language, power and agency as key factors in fashioning the future of England, and the wider world.

About Time

In 'Killing Time' the ghosts of the past do not reappear as mere reminders, but are reanimated in the present to illuminate their haunting inheritance. Offering a literary phantasmagoria of cultural icons from across the twentieth century, 'Killing Time' presents a millennial England that is haunted simultaneously by the ghosts of its past, present and future. Famous faces unite to offer a spectrally suggestive review of the relatively minor progress made by humanity since their passing. As imagined possibilities, the many specters of the poem do not function as remnants of a past time, but actively gesture towards the spectrality of being at the turn of the millennium. These imagined reanimations function to make visible the presence of the absent, demanding that, as readers, 'we reckon with what modern history has rendered ghostly',[15] avoiding complacency, passivity and acceptance, and instead encouraging us to become critical global citizens.

Charting the 'Chinese whisper of a countdown' (45) that 'spreads across the world' on New Year's Eve 1999, the poem reflects on the range and scale of events used to welcome in the new millennium, from large nationally organized displays and local street parties, to the 'millions' of people who are

> focused on keeping themselves to themselves,
>   determined to opt out,
> not to be moved by a fictional date and a fictional time. (46)

Across the poem, Armitage uses poetic structure to consider the nature of time at the end of a thousand years. In each stanza, time is represented as an enigma and is measured, kept and greeted in a variety of ways that combine to highlight the continuous change and speed that characterizes the contemporary moment. With its fast pace, staccato rhythms and run-on lines, 'Killing Time' is structurally suggestive of a relentless flow of time in the lead up to the millennium. Within this traumatic context, Armitage mobilizes symbolic human engagements with the natural world to highlight the ways in which time can be felt to stop, or pause, amidst the chaos of contemporary life.

During August 1999, a rare total solar eclipse occurred in England, as the moon crossed between the earth and the sun to create a finite moment of suspended time.[16] In the context of the late twentieth century, where 'more people worship the sun these days than God' (34), Armitage appropriates the 1999 solar eclipse as a moment of respite from hyper-visibility and an image conscious culture. Armitage presents this moment of time out-of-joint as an opportunity for humanity to consider its future direction and aspirations for the thousand years ahead. As the moon covers the sun in his poem, spectators witness 'time running backwards' (36) and feel 'a huge sense of time and space' (37). The suspended temporality of the eclipse becomes a spectral space in which people can pause their endless pursuit of material goods and 'come together', or 'at least as a race stop beating the shit out of each other' to instead

> try and make use or sense
> of what time we have left
>   bearing in mind the complete absence of anything else? (37)

The poem harnesses this occasion to foreground the concept of time as lived experience, one characterized by an awareness of change, events that have happened in the past, and events that are anticipated in the future. In a single moment of pause, the poet finds room for reflection, raising the natural world as a space free from the constraints and expectations of the pursuit of commercialization that he feels has come to define pre-millennial culture.

Time may be universally significant, but it is nevertheless conceptually abstract. As Laura A. Janda argues, 'time is perhaps the only feature of our existence which we all agree exists despite the fact that we have absolutely no direct evidence of its existence. We have no sensory perception of time whatsoever, we cannot see or hear or touch it, nor measure it directly. If time exists at all, it exists purely as an epiphenomenon of effects on ourselves and the things around us'.[17] In his millennial poem, Armitage uses the metaphor of water to make intelligible the abstraction of time. Fluid in its direction of flow, water has memory, and in 'Killing Time' it functions to reanimate the past in the present. The poem proposes that 'only water will work' to replicate 'the action of time', to engage in the process of 'conjuring up what is unseen and unsung' in 'a history smothered by dust', revealing

> everything locked in time's keep,
> everything buried, enshrined, encoded, entombed
> in sleep. (32)

Throughout the poem, water as memory is positioned as a paradox, 'the glue of time', or a type of

> gum that sets the past
>   in solid form, binding it shut,
> holding it monumentally hard and fast.
>   So history can be opened again,
> but not by force. (31)

Memory is shown to be discontinuous and porous, subject to an indefinable structure that operates between states of presence and absence. This dialectic flow suggests that while history offers facts, memory offers a vital alternative narrative. Creating an image of time not only in relation to the past hundred years, but to the past thousand, Armitage represents the 'time of the now'[18] and the tangle of 'historical fault lines that remain'[19] from history, to question the 'extent to which the past governs the present and opens or forecloses possibilities for the future'.[20]

Critically appraising the millennium as the end of history, 'Killing Time' tackles a newly emergent awareness of time, and a feeling of time passing, as well as a pervading sense of the inexorable march of humanity as it reaches the end of a century. The repeated image of 'history' as a 'tracking shot along railway lines' (25) is indicative of this tension between movement and progress as set against stasis and suffering. Juxtaposing the historical and the contemporary, Armitage combines images of the past and future with humour and horror to offer bleak and reflective summations on the last thousand years, as well as predictions about the future of mankind, and the planet.

No News Is Good News

In the years leading up to the new millennium, a host of technological innovations enabled an exponential growth in the scale and influence of the global news media. The second half of the twentieth century alone witnessed the rise of the internet, smart phones, and wireless technology. The increasingly spectral nature of this modern media produced a new state of 'insistent visibility' and 'a culture seemingly ruled by technologies of hypervisibility'.[21] Across 'Killing Time', the media and its absent subjects are implicitly connected to underscore the inherently spectral nature of the digital and virtual. Spectralizing streams of new media, Armitage critically frames the pervasive experience of haunting and the disconcerting lack of clarity between the real and unreal images offered by the many screens that feature throughout his poem. Inhabiting a 'phantom structure',[22] these new media technologies function to bring the spectral into everyday life, haunting the contemporary through a 'virtual space of spectrality'.[23]

Enabled by pre-millennial technological developments, television news launched a range of twenty-four hour news channels that aimed to break audiences away from their familiar daily news cycle. Concomitant with the increasingly fast-paced lifestyles of the millennial generation, new twenty-four hour news channels launched to create increased competition for viewers and advertising. Offering sophisticated graphics, permanent scrolling news messages, and uninterrupted live images from across the world, contemporary news channels aimed to offer compelling and non-stop 'breaking news' in order to satisfy a new desire for content. Journalists nick-named 'dish monkeys' were sent to far-flung locations and told to 'vamp'—a media term meaning to 'kill time' or fill dead air—while waiting for news to 'happen'. This new form of journalism effectively pitted the competing demands of profit and viewing figures against ethics and editorial judgement and was criticized for producing sensationalist entertainment rather than reporting what was relevant and researched. Media critic David Weaver argues that the advent of numerous competing twenty-four hour television news channels across this period in reality conspired to produce a 'journalism of assertion', one that focused less on whether a story was true, and more on introducing it into the field of public discussion as quickly as possible.[24] Although 'Killing Time' is largely fuelled by stories representing contemporary events, Armitage is overtly critical of the limitations of contemporary news media, arguing that

> my gut feeling is that news is just as much about what we don't know is going on, what doesn't find its way into our living room. We use the news as a barometer of the world, and it tells us how we're meant to feel that day. But there are issues of selection, presentation, authorial judgment. News is

business, and it ends as entertainment. Sometimes I find that stomach-churning.[25]

The illusion of choice offered by new twenty-four hour rolling news is exposed by his poem as producing a closed, linear channel of communication in which increasingly overblown stories are deliberately narrated in a manner that pleases the target demographic of the broadcaster.

In its opening lines, 'Killing Time' presents readers with a biological hybrid of Darwinian evolution in the form of a 'media monkey' specially adapted for the twenty-first century. Armitage's media-monkey draws attention to the strangeness of new media developments and traces its previous formations in the physical constitution of the ape. With a 'huge appetite' (3) for news, its corrupted evolutionary pattern produces a blank canvas on which events are ingested and projected. Educated and amplified by the media, the monkey stands as a symbol of the increasing mediation of experience in contemporary society. Recharged and reformatted for a new age, the part-animal, part-computer creature lacks the facilities and emotions that guide and define human responses. Instead, its talents lie in making visible every element of human life for consumption by the masses. A creature notable only for its internalized technology and insatiable desire for news, this 'money gone wrong' (3) is presented as both a literal and metaphorical 'part' of the media systems that govern it. Living only in the moment, the media-monkey eats news 'like there was no tomorrow' (3), has a penchant for 'anything live' and a notable 'thirst for sorrow' (4). Feeding on the sadness and trauma provided by a ceaseless flow of news events, the money is overwhelmed, and ultimately reduced to a state of inaction.

In 'Killing Time', the visibility propounded by the news media is combined with an authority that implies an absence of complexity or contradictions in the images being fed to the media-monkey. The poem sardonically highlights that the monkey can only manage simple narratives, and broad discourses, and needs 'meaty bits chopped up small' (4) to aid digestion. The final image of humans gathered at the monkey's feet, watching a vacuous 'news' broadcast (wryly described by Armitage as a 'visual fart'—4) chillingly aligns this Frankenstein creature with the condition of humanity at the turn of the century. As the monkey begins to 'sing' (4) a never-ending stream of news, his audience are placed in the position of passive consumers, apparently unconscious of the monkey-mechanism through which the media communicates to the masses.

'Killing Time' wryly opens with the claim that 'NO NEWS IS GOOD NEWS', but throughout the poem Armitage interrogates an emergent awareness of the consequences of new technological developments and twenty-four hour news on millennial society. The poem itself is structured to resemble a rolling news channel, with reports and dispatches from the front line punctuating a series of reports on the unfolding events of the year 1999, blurring boundaries between televisual simulacra and lived reality. Even the bloody Kosovo War (February 1998–June 1999) and its audible 'selection of human screams' (50) are physically drowned out by mass mediation through the auditory landscape of conflict projected by the news media. Distracted and eventually deafened by an orchestra of mobile phones, tape-recorders and cameras, soldiers gradually realize

> That interference jamming the air,
> that babble of white noise,
> that signal bending and burning the ears
> was the radiation of the news. (51)

Charting the creation of a state of insistent visibility in which new media technologies dominate communication, 'Killing Time' interrogates the spectral power of the media not only to hauntingly (re)present, but to actively create conflict, even in a war zone.

ONE WORD FROM WAR

Simon Armitage is perhaps best known as a poet for his humour and wit. However, 'Killing Time' marks a change in his use of satire as the poetic is mobilized to highlight a critical perspective on the rise of violent conflict in the contemporary period. The poem situates its millennial 'tribute' in an emerging context of human disaster and war. Armitage reflects that his representation of conflict in poetry, is partly 'a reaction' to his time spent working 'as a probation officer in Manchester' before he became a full time poet.[26] He uses

> violence in poems to make contact with other human beings. I felt that we were pretty sleepy as a species, and that a good jolt of a primitive human emotion could do the trick of waking people up. I also think there is an element there of growing up in the Thatcher years in the 70s and 80s, which were particularly violent times. In later poems, even though that violence is still there, it is more mediated. I think that is what is going on

[in Killing Time]. It is still prevalent, but maybe I am digging it out of the classical sources. I see it as war rather than personal violence, but there is a connection between the two—if you can't get it right in town, you're not going to get it right across international boundaries.[27]

Offering the crimes of the time as a social metaphor indicative of the wider moral decay of culture at the moment of the year 2000, 'Killing Time' raises a series of violent encounters to generate a critique of conflicts active across the globe during the millennial period.

Domestic English hate crimes are represented by the poem in a short stanza concerning the 1999 Soho bombings. From 17–24 April 1999 a series of bombs exploded across London, killing and injuring hundreds of people. The sites of the explosions—Brixton, Brick Lane, and the Admiral Duncan pub on Old Compton Street, Soho—targeted well-known sites in the city's gay scene. Armitage's poem reflects that

> This season, luggage containing terrible thoughts
> was left in Brixton, Soho and Brick Lane
> the kind which scatters the baggage of one man's mind
> into the public brain. (28)

Replacing nails with 'thoughts', his poem foregrounds the attacks as political acts and raises the specter of homophobia as a persistent problem as the year 2000 approaches. Framing the haunting image of there being 'something in the mind', the poem spectrally connects the various violent acts across its stanzas.

Re-presenting infamous international events that came to define the year 1999, Armitage revisits well-known stories from a poetic perspective in an attempt to offer an alternative view on humanity at the end of the century. Divisions at home and abroad litter his stanzas, while internal divisions within the 'United Kingdom' are reinforced through references to devolution in Scotland and Wales, and the burgeoning context of the Good Friday Agreement in Northern Ireland (finally brought into effect in December 1999). The image of St Nicholas looming over the map of England 'bent double with the heavy pillow-case of peace in Ireland' (7) anchors the text to a climate of intensity and anxiety, as the gift of peace which, although delivered, remains to be opened as the end of the century approaches.

Through its critique of violent aggression in England and beyond, the poem offers a stark warning concerning the safety of civilization as it enters the new millennium. Satirizing Christmas celebrations as thinly veiled distractions from conflicts overseas ('the bright star over the Middle East' does not signal the virgin birth but 'the burn of a cruise missile homing in', 5) and an increasing surveillance society, 'Killing Time' satirizes the special relationship between the US and England, foregrounding the conflicts that define the era and reminding contemporary readers that

> however far
>   we think we might have come, we are still only
> One word from war. (6)

The impact on England of violent events overseas is critically examined in one of the longest sections of 'Killing Time' that re-presents the worst high school shootings in American history. The events that became widely known as the 'Columbine High School Massacre' occurred in April 1999 at Columbine High School in Colorado, USA. The attack comprised two waves—an initial slaying of teachers and fellow pupils by the two teenage male killers, and a second organized series of fire bombs and explosive devices planted around the school to prevent police and the army accessing the site. Even though the attack occurred in a relatively small high school in America, events quickly became an iconic feature of global news media, as pictures of the crime scene and interviews with survivors were swiftly captured by on-location television news and beamed around the world.[28]

Armitage reimagines these notorious shootings through an elegiac accolade in which flowers, rather than bullets, are used by the 'two boys' to offer 'floral tributes to fellow students and members of staff, beginning with red roses' (22). Events unfold 'somewhere in the state of Colorado' (22), and are quickly broadcast nationwide. Initial public responses to the shootings betray a wider culture of simulation propounded by the news media, as 'most thought the whole show was one elaborate hoax', involving 'replicas' and 'imitations' (22) more familiar to television news dramas. In fact, the boys and their guns prove to be 'no more fake than you or I' (22) and it is the authentic nature of the drama unfolding live on television screens that leads members of the public and news media to the scene. Like the media-monkey that opens the poem, the growing Columbine crowds feed off the sadness of the news—'like hummingbirds dipping their tongue in' the grief and trauma of the massacre, they 'savour the goings-on' (23) long after the killers have taken their own lives.

The use of images from the natural world—flowers, birds, butterflies and fruits—transposed on to a massacre creates a distancing from events and draws critical attention to the appearance and reality of 'two apparently quiet kids' (23) who chose to take the lives of their classmates and teachers. Ending with a reflection on the right to bear arms outlined by the American constitution, 'Killing Time' satirizes the reality of gun culture through its spectrally haunting floral tributes, using nature to move away from the specificity of debates about gun laws and towards more profound and pressing moral and ethical questions resonant to humanity at the end of a thousand years. The nature/nurture question, 'is it something in the mind that grows from birth, like a seed, or is it society makes a person that kind?' (24) is left hanging at the end of the poem, implicating both the news media and the public in their co-creation of deviance.

Through the provocative title, 'Killing Time', Armitage quickly establishes the pre-millennial period as a time in which killing is prevalent, and conflicts multiple. In his poem, the unresolved traumas of the recent past return to compound the conflicts of the present, contextualizing current aggression against a history of cyclical confrontation. The structure of the poem closely mimics that of an extended elegy for these many battles, mobilizing traditional elegiac symbols in its criticism of both national and international hostilities. The unsettling specters of these disputes return to disrupt the present, creating tension in a moment of millennial celebration to offer a counter-narrative on the past through their haunting afterlife. In their resurgence, these specters highlight the need to move forwards in awareness of, and dialogue with the past, in order to continue the evolution of civilization and to avoid the repetition of former conflicts. Rather than 'killing' the time of the past, Armitage's millennial poem encourages a new appreciation of its role in the present, through a range of historical specters that contribute new understandings and contexts to the forward-facing moment of the year 2000.

FUTURE TIME

Almost two decades after it was written, the millennial anxieties that haunt 'Killing Time' remain more relevant than ever. The poem offers both a warning of what is to come, and a future facing prediction that

> the thing we were told
> was a thing of the past is coming up once more like the dawn,
> and it is dark, and it is cold. (7)

The core thesis of the poem—that the past has a direct bearing on the events of the present and future, and cannot simply be laid to rest as the new century begins—implies that in order to understand present day conflict, conditions and contradictions, it is necessary to listen to the spectral presence of the past, and to recognize it as an active force that is constantly engaged in making inroads into the present moment, and incursions in the future. The paradox of recognizing the competing ties of history, and the desire for a new start for the next millennium, is interrogated through the many commemorative activities profiled by the poem that draw critical attention to reiterations of history, and a human compulsion to endlessly repeat and revisit marginalized or overlooked occasions as an act of retrieval. Presenting its various historical recontextualizations as acts of resurrected haunting, Armitage enables his specters to enter the visible world of the present through the disjointed temporality constructed by the poetic form.

Despite the daunting nature of the events it describes, 'Killing Time' is optimistic in its suggestion that there remains time to change, for humanity to reject consumption, corporate greed and media domination, and to harness technological progress and globalization for a wider human good. In a moment of respite from the chaos and conflict of the year preceding the millennium, the poem pauses to reflect that 'more and more people are climbing mountains in Iceland these days' (12) in an attempt to escape from the new media vortex and to re-engage with the natural world. As 'Messrs Piccard and Jones' (17) drift above the earth in their hot air balloon, the poet is inspired to imagine a twenty-first century world with 'invisible borders' (18) in which no human is 'tied to any plot of land' but is instead 'aerial and detached' (19) as a cosmopolitan citizen of the world. In such a context, it is possible to hope that 'wounds heal, battlefields go to pot, weapons to rust' (20). Although this flight of fancy is immediately undermined as 'Impossible of course', the repeated rhetorical question 'but couldn't we just, couldn't we just?' (20) remains unresolved in the poem's closing lines.

Through its spectral intrusions, 'Killing Time' suggests that the future is only possible if we confront the non-contemporaneity of the present moment and 'learn to live with ghosts'[29] from the recent past. Calling forth a new knowledge from the shadows of historical record, this haunting affect encourages a new awareness, since 'haunting recognition is a special way of knowing what has happened or what is happening'.[30] In their fleeting sense of actuality, the many specters of the poem function to 're-establish a dynamic connection between past and future',[31] a spectral inheritance that speaks as much of the present and future as it does of the past. As a series of repetitions, they collectively produce a dead image of futural time, one that is reflective of the perceived relative interiority of the present and the insularity of current progress. Highlighting the 'persistence of the past in the present',[32] 'Killing Time' encourages a critical consideration of both the concept of time, and its relationship to our understandings of the past.

Representing the millennial moment as a phantasmal time haunted by compulsive historical returns, Armitage considers how and why the moment of the millennium is disjointed by the intrusion of the past which emerges as a spectral inheritance. Considering the legacies of this past on individual, national and global scales, 'Killing Time' interrogates the burden of history, as well as the ways in which the contemporary disavows this burden. Across the poem, spectral events reappear as a sign of the vexed relationship between time and memory, offering a creative and critical counterpoint to current time, and a challenge to the privileging of the future. Profiling spectral pasts uncannily brought back to life as the year 2000 approaches, 'Killing Time' critically explores the extent to which the past controls the present and creates possibilities for the future.

Encouraging a spectral reading of the present, Armitage's millennial specters highlight the hidden and indirect ways that the past continues to linger and manifest itself. While they do not offer any easy solutions to the problems posed by the poem, these specters do propose alternative political and ontological frameworks through which contemporary readers can choose to understand the power of time and memory. Spectral traces resurrect past preoccupations that haunt millennial society as shadows of a history that rejects closure and continues to resonate with the present time. Retro-activating the past in the present, specters encourage past and present to collide, and so disturb millennial consciousness and heterogeneous celebrations of the countdown to millennium eve.

As a popular phrase, 'Killing Time' is often understood to mean a mundane act used to pass time aimlessly, or to keep busy while waiting for something else to happen. In Armitage's poem, the phrase takes on new political and social meanings, as well as evolutionary implications for humanity. Trapped between mourning for the past, and anxiety for the future, humanity is represented in a state of stasis that positions the horizon of the new millennium not as a promising new dawn, but as an uncompromising spotlight on unresolved conflicts at the turn of the century.

Using literary form as 'a framing device for experience',[33] Armitage demonstrates the potential of poetry to capture emergent structures of feeling generated in response to a period of temporal transition. Critiquing a thousand years of Western culture and civilization in a thousand lines of poetic verse, in 'Killing Time' leitmotifs of war, social class, poverty and violent crime conspire to raise the shared spectral dynamics of writing and memory. Offering new poetic perspectives on the events that produced headlines in the media across 1999, Armitage uses his official millennial commission to suggest that history remains our greatest enemy, and our greatest ally, in shaping the future.

NOTES

1. Simon Armitage, *Killing Time* (London: Faber and Faber, 1999).
2. A 'millennium' is widely understood as a period of time equal to one thousand years, or a 'kiloyear'. Since the Western Gregorian calendar begins with a number 1, each period of a thousand years concludes with a date that ends in 000. However, in the astronomical calendar the year starts at 0, and consequently there were international debates in the year 1999 about whether the beginning of the year 2000 should or should not be celebrated as marking the 'beginning' of the millennium.
3. Charles B. Strozier, *The Year 2000: Essays on the End* (London: New York University Press, 1997) p. 2.
4. Strozier, 1997, p. 5.
5. Frank Kermode, *The Sense of an Ending: Studies in the Theory of Fiction* (New York: Open University Press, 1967) pp. 95–96.
6. Don DeLilo, *Mao II* (New York: Viking, 1991) p. 80.
7. Erected in October 1999, the London Eye is a 125 metre tall landmark that surpasses the height of other, more famous, features of the London skyline including Big Ben and St Paul's Cathedral. In 'Killing Time', this landmark of the millennium is represented as little more than a political tool, 'powered by hot air and other parliamentary emissions' that are 'piped up' from the parliament building on the opposite bank of the River Thames in London.
8. Andrew Motion also penned a poem to commemorate the turn of the millennium in 1999. The finished work—'2000: Zero Gravity: The Millennium Report'—was published in the English daily newspaper *The Guardian*, <https://www.theguardian.com/books/1999/dec/27/poetry.millennium>
9. Simon Armitage quoted in Alex Macdonald, 'Jaundiced Reality: Simon Armitage Interviewed', *The Quietus*, 12 October 2014 <http://thequi-

etus.com/articles/16464-simon-armitage-paper-aeroplanes-interview-next-generation-poetry>

10. *Killing Time* was adapted as a made-for-television film screened on New Year's Day, 1 January 2000 on English television station Channel 4. The adaptation offers a more straightforward narrative, one that follows the progress of 'Millennium Man', a kind of everyman protagonist, as he travels through England collecting objects from the past that have been forgotten or ignored. The central narrative of the film is interspersed with footage of real people surrendering their own memory objects from the past thousand years, culminating in a final and symbolic pyre, burning memory and time, at the Millennium Dome in Greenwich, London, the Prime Meridian of Greenwich from which time around the world is measured.

11. Simon Armitage quoted in Robert Potts, 'Mean Time', *The Guardian*, 15 December 1999 <https://www.theguardian.com/books/1999/dec/15/poetry.artsfeatures>

12. Simon Armitage quoted in Robert Potts, 'Mean Time', *The Guardian*, 15 December 1999 <https://www.theguardian.com/books/1999/dec/15/poetry.artsfeatures>

13. Simon Armitage quoted in Alex Macdonald, 'Jaundiced Reality: Simon Armitage Interviewed', *The Quietus*, 12 October 2014 <http://thequietus.com/articles/16464-simon-armitage-paper-aeroplanes-interview-next-generation-poetry>

14. Simon Armitage quoted in Alex Macdonald, 'Jaundiced Reality: Simon Armitage Interviewed', *The Quietus*, 12 October 2014 <http://thequietus.com/articles/16464-simon-armitage-paper-aeroplanes-interview-next-generation-poetry>

15. Gordon, 2008, p. 18.

16. Due to the high population of the areas featured in the path of totality, this natural spectacle became one of the most-viewed total solar eclipses in human history. Many people organized eclipse-watching parties, or set up video projectors to record the event. The occasion of the solar eclipse is presented by the news media as a natural wonder, one prime for mediation and authentic experience, with pictures of the eclipse shadow beamed live from the Mir Space station.

17. Laura A. Janda, 'The conceptualization of events and their relationship to time in Russian', *Glossos*, Issue 2, Winter 2002. p. 3.

18. Walter Benjamin, 1969, p. 263

19. Gordon: 2008, p. 139.

20. Jeffrey Weinstock (ed.), *Spectral America: Phantoms and the National Imagination* (London: University of Wisconsin Press, 2004) p. 8.

21. Gordon: 2008, p. 15–16.

22. Derrida, 1989, p. 61
23. Derrida, 1994, p. 11.
24. David Weaver (ed.) *The American Journalist in the 21st Century: U.S. News People at the Dawn of a New Millennium* (New York: Routledge, 2006) p. 226.
25. Simon Armitage quoted in Robert Potts, 'Mean Time', *The Guardian*, 15 December 1999 <https://www.theguardian.com/books/1999/dec/15/poetry.artsfeatures>
26. Simon Armitage quoted in Alex Macdonald, 'Jaundiced Reality: Simon Armitage Interviewed', *The Quietus*, 12 October 2014 <http://thequietus.com/articles/16464-simon-armitage-paper-aeroplanes-interview-next-generation-poetry>
27. Simon Armitage quoted in Alex Macdonald, 'Jaundiced Reality: Simon Armitage Interviewed', *The Quietus*, 12 October 2014 <http://thequietus.com/articles/16464-simon-armitage-paper-aeroplanes-interview-next-generation-poetry>
28. In the aftermath there was international debate about the motivations of the killers and the extent to which the attack could have been prevented. 'Columbine' became part of the common vernacular when referring to school shootings, and the killings even spawned an online fan culture of fellow discontents who termed themselves 'Columbiners'.
29. Derrida, 1994, p. xviii.
30. Gordon, 2008, p. 63.
31. Pierre Macherey, 'Marx Dematerialised, or the Spirit of Derrida' in Michael Sprinker (ed.) *Ghostly Demarcations: A Symposium on Jacques Derrida's Specters of Marx* (London: Verso, 2008) p. 19.
32. Esther Peeren, *The Spectral Metaphor: Living Ghosts and the Agency of Invisibility* (London: Palgrave Macmillan, 2014) p. 10.
33. Simon Armitage quoted in Alex Macdonald, 'Jaundiced Reality: Simon Armitage Interviewed', *The Quietus*, 12 October 2014 <http://thequietus.com/articles/16464-simon-armitage-paper-aeroplanes-interview-next-generation-poetry>

Phantasmal Intertexts: Literary Spectrality in Jez Butterworth's *Jerusalem* (2009)

Abstract This chapter explores the haunting use of intertextuality in Butterworth's 2009 stage drama *Jerusalem*. It considers how the play ingests exterior texts in its narrative of the present and why it frequently repeats symbolic representations through citation and reference. The paradox highlighted by these intertextual returns captures the difference and sameness, the recognizable uncanny, in the every day. In considering how and why intertextual subjects emerge again in Butterworth's most successful drama, the chapter surveys extensive meta-textual connectivities to examine the function of intertextual haunts on the contemporary English stage.

Keywords Play • Drama • Jez Butterworth • Spectral • Contemporary • Stage • Intertextual • England • Absence • Uncanny

Since the turn of the new century, a new generation of English playwrights has been experimenting with the dramatic form to respond to and represent the challenges of contemporary society. The products of these experiments are a range of 'disrupted narratives'[1] that harness the spectral to represent the tumultuous social, political and economic contexts facing the twenty-first century. Ghosts have proved popular subjects on the English stage, but in theatre produced after the year 2000, the popularity of ghosts not only continued, but exploded.[2] This uncanny influx led theatre critic Sophie Nield to use her 2009 *Guardian* newspaper column to reflect that 'the long and eerie tradition of stage ghosts is experiencing

© The Author(s) 2018
K. Shaw, *Hauntology*,
https://doi.org/10.1007/978-3-319-74968-6_3

another rebirth'. Considering why English theatre was 'so fascinated with the spectral'[3] in the first decade of the new millennium, Nield asked 'what is it about theatrical culture that tends so much towards the ghostly?'[4]

Jez Butterworth's 2009 drama *Jerusalem* is haunted by the pervading presence of a series of intertextual ghosts that function to extend the influence of events on stage, enabling his contemporary drama to stage debates about English culture and identity in the post-millennial period. Using haunting to draw attention to the repetitious power of writing, Butterworth extends the agency of the spectral intertext beyond the past, into the present moment and forward to a future that his characters still have the chance to shape. Harnessing phantasmal hauntings, Butterworth confronts contemporary audiences with the reality of post-millennium problems: disengagement, marginalization and the apparent impossibility of collective action. Transposing myth and motif on to a changing pastoral setting, *Jerusalem* takes tales and images from England's past to highlight their informative influence on the country's future.

Intertextuality constitutes an integral structural feature of *Jerusalem*, a play whose literary echoes generate a network of hauntings and revisitations that highlight visibility, representation and performativity as central critical concerns. These self-conscious intertextualities are openly referenced through the title and dialogue of the play, allowing directed spectral revivals to occur on the stage. Intertexts also disrupt the linear progression of literary history, demanding a critical re-visioning of the canon and its continued relevance in the contemporary period. Introducing haunting as a dramaturgical structure through which the agency of the past in the present can be exercised to trace invisibility and presence on the stage, Butterworth's twenty-first century English drama forges new connections between texts and pre-texts, intertextual patterns and the phantasmal hauntings of Butterworth's twenty-first century English drama.

GREEN AND PLEASANT LAND

The poem 'Jerusalem' was originally written by William Blake as a preface to *Milton: An Epic* in 1808. It articulated a sense of loss and of time passing at the point of the industrial revolution, and reflected on the impact of this development on English society. Set to music in 1916 by composer Hubert Parry to encourage patriotism and a nationalistic spirit during war-time, its words consider the possibility of a second coming by Jesus to earth (specifically to England) and debate whether such a visit would create a new heaven, on English soil. Butterworth's play offers a direct intertextual reference to Blake's poem, opening with a musical rendition of two complete stanzas:

> And did those feet in ancient time,
> Walk upon England's mountains green,
> And was the holy Lamb of God,
> On England's pleasant pastures seen.
> And did the Countenance Divine,
> Shine forth upon our clouded hills,
> And was Jerusalem builded here,
> Among these dark satanic—(5)

Across Blake's poem, images of a new heaven are set against the 'dark satanic mills' of the Victorian industrial revolution to critique its impact on the human and natural worlds. 'Jerusalem' is established as a state of mind as much as a place, a point at which the many divisions and disagreements of the world are resolved, and society is united behind a common national identity.

In the years following the publication of Blake's poem, his vision of a 'green and pleasant' land became a byword for nostalgic perspectives on the English countryside. While Blake's poetic devices may appear to point towards nostalgia and even patriotism, they also mobilize irony to critique the pressure exercized by the propertied classes on the working classes of the nineteenth century. Blake wrote against the repression of the individual and the censoring of the self, instead promoting resistance and protest, and advocating the 'mental fight' of the individual against the state. Butterworth draws upon this history of resistance, using Blake as an inspiration for his contemporary stage drama *Jerusalem*. Set on St George's Day (an annual day of celebration for England's patron saint) and the day of the county fair, both the opening scene and title of Butterworth's play draw heavily on references to Blake. However, Butterworth reframes Blake's four central questions regarding the challenges of coping with a changing sense of national identity and the loss of public space. Highlighting connections between a shared past and the pressing changes of the contemporary moment, Butterworth's *Jerusalem* presents a contextually informed 'haunting study of a changing England',[5] using spectrality as a mode through which to stage the politics of disenfranchisement, nostalgia, localism and nationalism.

Written at a turning point between the end of one century and the start of another, *Jerusalem* grapples with the difficulty of trying to make sense of the potentially transformative power of loss. Through a series of 'losses'—the loss of the countryside, the loss of individuality and the loss of alternative lifestyles and cultures—the play questions national identity and the relationship between the individual and the state in twenty-first century England. In doing so, Butterworth's drama reveals the more subtle intertextual power of Blake's poem 'Jerusalem' in shaping its own dramatic representations of the spectral role of the past in contemporary English culture. Although Butterworth claims it was 'never my intention to write something about the state of the nation',[6] *Jerusalem* is very much a play about the state of England at the beginning of the twenty-first century and the author's own 'sense of loss and [...] attitudes towards change'.[7]

The setting of *Jerusalem* can be read as part of a wider shift in twenty-first century English drama 'away from the metropolitan centre' towards a concern with representing 'rural geographical sites, cultural idioms, local histories and heritage that exist way beyond London'.[8] Butterworth often locates his plays in edgelands, those spaces on the outskirts of towns, 'not meant to be seen'.[9] His settings suggest the presence of an 'overlooked England' at the margins of our known geographies. Although deceptively simple, these dramatic settings often constitute places in which individuals are free from obligation, expectation and profession. Set apart from the regulations and confines of civil and civic society, in *Jerusalem* the woods represent an unchartered space that is removed from the rules of the everyday. Growing from 'English soil' (9), the woods command a spectral position in relation to the town, and inspire mystic associations in the popular consciousness of its inhabitants. Lee claims that 'there's a ley line runs clean through this wood. Clean through this copse. Ley lines is lines of ancient energy, stretching across the landscape. Linking ancient sites [...]. This is holy land' (72). As a social specter, Johnny uses the woods to observe from a distance the world around him. Through a Derridean 'visor effect', he maintains surveillance over everything in the forest, from the foxes and badgers of the woods, to runaway lovers and girls giving birth behind trees: 'I've seen a lot of strange things in this wood [...] Ghosts. I've seen a lot of ghosts. (*Beat*) I seen women burn love letters. Men dig holes in the dead of night. I seen a young girl walk down here in the cold dawn, take all her clothes off, wrap her arms round a broad beech tree and give birth to a baby boy. I seen all the world pass by and go'

(102). The teenagers who 'haunt' his forest kingdom are drawn there in their quest to locate an alternative to the sanitized regularity of their suburban lives and a different landscape to the ones offered by their urban dwellings.

In choosing to set his drama not only in the countryside, but also against the backdrop of a local county fair, Butterworth signals an early interest in profiling the politically spectral. As the Professor reveals, the tradition of the county fair can be traced back to 1521 as 'a time for revelry [...] to be free from constraint. A time to commune with the flora and the fauna of this enchanted isle. To abandon oneself to the rhythms of the earth' (52). The county fair caters to a particular demand in English culture for the celebration of the local, and the confirmation of community identity. In the time of Butterworth's play this demand remains, but the county fair has become sterilized and commodified, sponsored and corporatized by a range of commercially interested parties. Instead of floats profiling the highlights of rural life, there is now 'a George and the Dragon. Men in Black II. Crown and Goose have gone X Factor' (19). The fair's floats and entertainment are sponsored and branded with corporate insignia. This is, claims Wesley, 'the brewery's idea. They've got right behind the fair this year. Point-of-sale material. T-shirts. Flintock Men. Special ale' (35). Even the signifier 'county fair' has been rebranded as 'The Annual St George's Day Pageant and Wessex Country Fair in the Village of Flintock sponsored by John Deere Tractors and Arkell Ales' (46). Rather than spontaneous displays of local skill, the occasion is now strictly programmed with a series of pre-planned 'festivities' (46) designed to draw upon the past to sell more merchanise in the present.

A famous historical feature of this occasion for carnival, Ginger reflects that, in years gone by, 'Johnny Byron *was* the Flintock Fair [...] People came from Berkshire, Dorset, Somerset, just to see him [...] He was a daredevil. Used to jump buses on a trials bike [...] Then, at the Flintock Fair, 1981, he died [...] He tried to jump twenty eighteen-wheelers, and he fucked it up, and he died' (31). This is the only story about Johnny that is confirmed by independent sources as well as by Johnny himself, suggesting a foundation for both his ego and conflict with authority when the 'Council stepped in' and 'made daredevilling illegal' (32). These tales of his former glories only serve to underline a growing sense in the play that 'the past does indeed initially seem to be a different country, or state of mind, with a heartless consumerist commercial modernity disrupting tradition and mystery'.[10]

It is possible to read numerous intertextual sources informing the character of Johnny. He exhibits elements of the mythic Green Man, of Robin Hood, the classical Pan and the Shakespearean Puck, Falstaff and Prospero. While Butterworth claims that the numerous Shakespearean influences and allusions that occur across *Jerusalem* were created 'by accident', 'unconscious' and 'completely by chance',[11] they collectively combine to produce a ghosting effect that raises an impoverished rural England still haunted by its ancient myths and almost subliminally trapped between the forces of old and new, chaos and officialdom. As well as channelling the literary heritage of the trickster, Johnny's provocative statement that 'whatever people say I am that's what I'm not' also raises intertextual specters of the English Angry Young Men dramas and fictions of the 1950s and 60s, contextualizing a vision of Butterworth's twenty-first century protagonist as an aged Jimmy Porter—an angry, if not young, man who is socially alienated, frustrated, and intent upon haunting a society that refuses to engage with his anger. Johnny's absence from the county fair in Butterworth's play, contrasted with the legend of his centrality to county fairs in years gone by, positions 'the missing' as an active force of resistance in the present.[12]

Absent Presence

The dramas of Jez Butterworth are concerned with what is missing, and what returns. Influenced by earlier English dramatists, *Jerusalem* includes intertextual nods to the works of Harold Pinter (*The Room*, 1960; *Moonlight*, 1993; *Ashes to Ashes*, 1996), Sarah Kane (*Blasted*, 1995; *Phaedra's Love*, 1996) and debbie tucker green (*Random*, 2008). By incorporating these influences, the play suggests an interest in capturing absence as well as in welcoming the ghost onto the contemporary stage. Butterworth argues that 'one of the first missions of the theatre is to allow a space where the voice of the dead can be heard'.[13] His is what Peter Brooks might call the 'Theatre of the-Invisible-made-visible'[14], that which offers a vision of what happens when the displaced return and force the contemporary to confront the uncanny. Johnny claims to have settled in the woods because it is an uncanny space, one that already felt familiar to him: 'I thought, "I know this place. Feels like I've been here before"' (102). This notion of the return is extended across the play as a structural concern with repetition, in returns to previous places, and the re-use of old items in the light of new knowledge or events.

Offering subversive approaches and departures from received perspectives on the past, *Jerusalem* is shaped by repeated references that function to subvert motifs and create structural echoes. A range of objects including Johnny's 'old Wessex flag', a sign that reads 'Waterloo' (6) and a drum are revisited throughout the play, enabling their significance to themes of nationalism, identity and conflict to grow in relation to each act of the return. These structurally uncanny revisitations serve to disrupt and fracture the seemingly naturalistic surface and setting of the play, as the return of significant objects and symbols creates a wider sense of time and place beyond the immediate confines of the dramatic structure. Butterworth's plays offer a radical and revisionary approach to time and space, offering an experience of pastoral temporality that is markedly different to city time. Trapped in his self-preserved stasis in the woods, Johnny experiences a different, slower sense of time. His ex-partner Dawn calls Johnny 'a stopped fucking clock', and reminds him of the need to 'Wake up' (66) and engage with the contemporary world. In a final altercation, she reminds him that 'the world turns. And it turns. And it moves on and you don't. You're still here' (66).

The county fair suspends accepted regulations of time, allowing characters to act outside of time constraints, expectations or requirements and even to absent themselves from society altogether during this period of celebration. This timeframe, intertextually established by Blake's poem, also suspends the authority of linear time associated with formal society, drawing attention to movements in space and time through the dramatic action. The concept of time is initially referenced by council officer Fawcett who underlines the importance of 'Time' (7) in the opening scene, and requests from Johnny 'a moment of your time' (7). The dramatic time of the play is marked by an increasing urgency and sense of time running out, especially for Johnny, with his impending eviction and the seizure of his home, but also with the imminent emigration of Lee to Australia on a 'dreamquest' of escape and adventure, and the final hours in the tenure of missing May Queen, Phaedra.

Missing characters exert a powerful haunting function in *Jerusalem*. Their absent presence signals a lack of meaning and control, but also hints at additional and contradictory forms of knowledge, experience and time. In their distinct dialectic of visibility and invisibility, the disappeared and the missing collapse certainties and charge the reality of the play with a new debt of inheritance. In doing so, they also create a haunting recognition of the significance of what is not being inherited by the next generation of fair-goers. The missing create a sense of time passing and mark a material presence despite their physical absence, suggesting that although they may be deprived of physical impact, the missing live on through their spectral agency. In *Jerusalem,* the missing return to destabilize present events and to encourage new perspectives on the past. These offstage characters conjure the presence of absence—manipulating their invisibility, they create shifts in meaning and new perspectives on dispossession. Mourning the absent, the characters in the play attempt to negotiate a reality defined by the paradoxical hypervisibility of the disappeared.

At the heart of *Jerusalem*—a play that is otherwise overwhelmingly immediate in its representations—lies the absence of Phaedra. Like a specter, she is paradoxically present and absent, replaced on stage by a series of traces and descriptions. Performing this absence, her character is missing yet multiple, reappearing at three distinct temporal markers in the dramatic structure. In doing so, she achieves a temporally destabilizing effect, injecting an enigmatic dynamic into the play. Phaedra is talked about but never seen in the dramatic action until the end of Act Two. Her absence leads to a fragmentation of meaning and possibility, as well as raising doubts about Johnny's character. Pointing to gaps and unresolved conflicts that are formative in the creation of new possibilities, the shifting and spectral presence of Phaedra draws attention to the ways in which absence operates across the play as both a latent threat, and as an anxiety experienced by other characters.

Phaedra is named after a Greek royal who falls in love with her step-son and, when spurned by him, accuses him of rape. Her presence on stage at the beginning of Butterworth's play contributes an anticipative intertextual haunt to the dramatic action, building the suspense of events to follow. Phaedra is initially offered as the opening host, appearing alone on stage before the start of Act One under the banner 'THE ENGLISH STAGE COMPANY' (5) singing *a capella* Blake's poem 'Jerusalem'. She appears on stage to deliver this prologue dressed as a fairy—an outfit later revealed to be the fancy dress outfit that prompted her ejection from local nightclub 'The 'Rakers' for being under age. This disagreement makes her run 'off into the night' (28) and disappear from view for most of the rest of the play. Davey 'reckons she's been got by a werewolf' (28), but her fleeting spectral appearances at the openings of Acts One and Two, against the sonic backdrop of Barry Dransfield's song 'Werewolf', gives a hauntological dimension to her absent presence. In fact, Phaedra the May Queen, spends much of the play contained in Johnny's trailer and, as such, is the subject of debate and conflict. Beyond her rare appearances on stage, the audience is only made aware of Phaedra by frequent references to her absence and through constant questions about where she might be. The tension caused by her disappearance continues to haunt the drama until her re-apparition at the close of Act Two when she emerges '*Shaking. Trembling. Shallow breathing*' (71) from Johnny's trailer. The status of the May Queen and her whereabouts remain ambiguous and unsettling, and raises uncomfortable questions about earlier events on stage, as well as about the spectral identities of the various individuals that move through the forest.

Conducting a critique via her absence, Phaedra demonstrates the ways in which the materiality of performance can foreground the significance of the missing. Since much of her presence is created through inference and the unsettling use of absence and double meaning, the pervading presence of her spectral threat encourages a new awareness of the ways in which visibility and power are interconnected. Destabilizing time, space and power through her missing body, Phaedra's un-dead and problematic spectrality critically and emotionally implicates Johnny, and the audience, in her continued concealment. Setting the disorder of the forest against the controlled and civilized housing estate, Butterworth positions Johnny's home and its spectralization of the 'missing' May Queen as antithetical to the territorial control and order desired and enacted by the council and the State. In her absence, Phaedra highlights not only the power of the missing over the community that searches for them, but also the political position of the wood as a liminal space, and Johnny as a socially marginalized 'Other' who is physically and metaphorically sidelined by the developments of twenty-first century English society.

Progressive Patriot

The spectral identity of those displaced and ghosted by shifts in the 'green and pleasant land' of contemporary England are epitomized by Johnny, a man who resides alone, in a mobile home, on the fringes of a small town. As a progressive patriot—a man who attempts to occupy the role of a free-born Englishman in protest at twenty-first century progress—Johnny occupies a liminal state that draws attention to the watershed between the acceptable and unacceptable, desired and undesired, and between the disenfranchised and the free. His residence status is not official, nor is it sanctioned, and Johnny's contribution to the community is social, rather than economic. As a proud protagonist, Johnny first appears on stage '*pissing up against a tree, his back to us*' (10) before letting out '*a long, feral bellow; from the heart of the earth*' (10). Across the play, Johnny is variously termed 'magic' (78), 'a dangerous nutter they should put behind glass' (51), 'a Gyppo, pikey, maggot, snake, gypsy' and the 'lowest piece of shit in this forest' (80). Johnny rejects the trappings of a capitalist lifestyle of acquisition and accumulation, and his mobile home stands in stark opposition to the 'permanent state' (6) that has grown around it. Surrounded by the remnants of the past—'An old hand-cranked air raid siren', 'an old submarine klaxon', 'an old record player' and 'an old American style fridge' (6)—his home is littered with historical leftovers. A local legend who, according to Ginger, 'slaughtered a live pig in the car park [...] With a flare gun', Johnny claims that 'All Byron boys come with their own cloaks' (49) and spends much of the play hiding behind a multiplicity of self-constructed images. As part of his own myth-making, Johnny claims to have been 'Born one day early and I've been a day ahead of all you beggars ever since' (50). Lee calls him 'Wiltshire's Biggest Bullshitter'" (33), while Tanya believes 'They should put him in the town square. Next to King Arthur' (33). Johnny's world is a fantasy construction of MI6 and lawyers in New York (24), of portraits commissioned by the Queen and a picture in the National Gallery (18). His double standards also mean that he can accuse others of exercising a 'diabolical liberty bordering on the criminal' (36) while he commits the same crimes, all the time claiming that 'there has to be rules' (39).

A vital representation of the power of wilderness and impermanence as set against the regulation of the state, Johnny's way of life offers a vital alternative narrative of ways of living in the twenty-first century. As a spectral figure, he defies categorization—he is not exactly of the white working classes that live in the local housing estate and town, but he is not exactly a Romany either since, as Phaedra points out, he doesn't actually travel anywhere. Johnny limps and struts, and he regularly shape shifts exhibiting the 'balance of a dancer, or an animal' (9). This ambiguity in a protagonist, coupled with his seemingly uncanny powers (as he looks into the eyes of another character, the wind gathers and the stage trembles), combine to underline his difference from the rest of the characters, and the audience. In his own words, Johnny is both the council's 'dreams and their worst nightmares' (24) because he cannot be understood, rationalized or resolved: his spectrality makes it impossible to fix him to a singular reading.

Johnny does not receive the hospitality of the local community but instead inspires fear, and is ostracized and demonized as a result of his difference. He offers a nexus of states, each of which lies beyond the received boundaries of the society he haunts. Johnny is a mirror that reflects the dark dimensions of the community and this uncomfortable reflection functions as a reminder that *Jerusalem* is not just about the failings of a single man, or a community group, but of a whole generation that has left behind some its most vulnerable people in a wider push for progress. In this capacity, the play illuminates a crisis of identity and purpose in twenty-first century England. Political journalist Andrew Marr has argued that the power of *Jerusalem* lies in its conscious decision to depict 'a rural England we all know is all around us, but hardly see on the stage'.[15] Questioning the control of English land, Butterworth foreshadows conflict within and beyond his play and validates the spiritual connections of place, as set against the economic rationalization of land as asset.

Initially, Johnny disregards his council eviction notice as a 'Storm in a teacup' (14). The ensuing battle for England's 'green and pleasant land' is one of ownership—it is either the revolutionary folk paradise of 'Rooster's Wood' (14), or a appropriated site of real estate development. Council officer Fawcett accuses Johnny of 'trespass' (94), 'attack' (95) and of being a 'drug dealer [...] to minors' (97). He judges his mobile home to be 'an illegal encampment' which has 'passed unchallenged since September 1982, a period of twenty-seven years, during which time no ground rent or rates have been paid to Kennet and Avon Council' (95). In his firm assertion that 'This land belongs to Kennet and Avon Council' (95), Fawcett directly contradicts Johnny's framing of the wood as a communal, shared space and raises the authority of 'The English law' in the form of a 'legally recognised petition of local complaints concerning the illegal encampment and activities hereabouts' (96).

At the end of the play, Johnny's rhetorical question 'What the fuck do you think an English forest is for?' (98), positions the woods as a site of liberation and escape. Johnny elevates his rebellion as 'a historic day' and supposes that 'in a thousand years, Englanders will awake this day and bow their heads and wonder at the genius, guts and guile of the Flintock Rebellion' (53). The Professor even attempts to frame Johnny's planned rebellion in the context of a long history of uprisings, arguing that 'English rebellions by their very nature are generally bloodthirsty affairs' (54). Despite this, The Flintock Rebellion, much like Johnny's game of Trivial Pursuit, ends up as a one man operation, 'all of you against me' (75), and it is Johnny who is finally held up as an example to others, branded on both cheeks and physically demarked as Other. The increasingly regular appearances of Spitfire planes crossing the sky (a spitfire flies over the stage at the opening of Act Three, then another (91), and finally again in the closing moments of the play) cumulatively builds anticipation of the invasion-to-come, reminding the audience of the spectral presence of the county fair, but also functioning metaphorically to evoke a 'blitz spirit' to Johnny's war with the council. Ginger's claim that 'They got an army. They're coming here' (105) and the threat that his 'camp will be razed, your vehicles and belongings will be seized as evidence' (97–8) motivates Johnny to curse the council officer to a spectral future, one in which he is doomed to 'wander the land forever' (108), condemned to experience Johnny's own spectral way of life.

The play concludes with a call to arms, but also with a rebirth. Alone, and deafened by the sound of beating, Johnny summons specters and stands waiting to meet giants: 'Come, you battalions. You fields of ghosts who walk these green plains still. Come, you giants!' (109). In these closing lines, Butterworth injects his drama with a final intertextual infusion of poetic and mythological allusion, alliteration and iambic pentameter evoking a Shakespearean level of gravity and tragedy, in the 'fields of ghosts' finally envisioned by his protagonist. Echoing Lee's earlier references to a Native American ritual of rebirth and freedom, Johnny performs 'an English ghost dance'[16] to ward off the arrival of the council officers. Johnny's final act of opposition to power can be read as an expression of a national 'determination to limit the authority of those who rule over us',[17] a very English trait. In the outward facing title of his play, Butterworth extends the questions and tensions originally raised by Blake and mobilizes them as a lens through which to consider debates of the contemporary. As a result, his play is 'ghosted by ancient questions, as much as it is by old, if not ancient, forms.[18] Challenging authority and authorship, control and meaning, Johnny's final inability to answer the Trivial Pursuit question 'Who wrote the words to the popular hymn "Jerusalem"?' (78) returns the dramatic narrative to its opening in Blake's original poem and contextualizes a call for answers to the questions about place, space, identity and agency, raised by Butterworth's later play.

Jerusalem makes visible formerly invisible people, lifestyles and perspectives that contemporary theatre rarely represents. Johnny and his band of merry men and women represent a culture on the precipice of being lost to the 'dark satanic mills' of twenty-first century progress. Butterworth

identifies this loss and change as key to understanding the political messages offered by his play. He adds: "For me, [...] It's about time and the
passing of time. It's about how for every single character in it, tomorrow
is going to be different to today. How you move from one state to another
is very difficult in life and I think a lot of people find it hard.'[19] Examining
the 'island mentality' of the English, his play presents eccentricity as a
mode that has become marginalized and discouraged in twenty-first century society. Johnny represents the loss of the local, of alternative narratives, others ways of being, the home-grown and the ancient as set against
the corporate and commercialized.

In the twenty-first century, Johnny's England has become 'this dark
place' (49), a heavily pasteurized version of England, in which marginal
locations and spectral characters are perceived as a threat to the efficient
operation of state power. Problematizing power relations through the
phantasmal presence of the questions raised by Blake's ancient intertext,
the play creates tensions through an exploration of the manifold ways in
which contemporary English culture is 'vulnerable at its margins'.[20]
Historically, St George's Day has been recognized as a day when the
nation confronts the monster that has been haunting it, a day of national
reckoning in which the dragon is slain and order restored. Finally it is the
council that answers the question raised in Phaedra's opening Prologue
about who owns and controls English land. The council cannot 'make the
wind blow' (98) as Johnny can, but they do ultimately exercise control
over the land, and over Johnny himself when they arrive on St George's
Day to slay the dragon-man who 'scorched the people with his breath'
(84).

Phantasmal Intertexts

As a contemporary critical engagement with Blake's earlier writing,
Butterworth's 2009 drama *Jerusalem* does not aim to put the ghosts of
Blake's poem to rest, but persistently raises them, even in its closing lines,
to deny resolution or clarity, and to disrupt the present through the intrusion of the past. Through the agency of the intertextual haunt, Butterworth
generates new meanings as well as implicit connections between past,
present and future. Reframing a carefully chosen source poem, his play
engages in a critical conversation and an act of destabilization, initiating a
simultaneous rereading of old and new writings. Situating the conflicts of
the present in a larger historical framework, his play suggests that the

issues addressed by Blake's original poem remain unresolved in the new millennium. Making the most familiar of national texts, 'Jerusalem', uncanny, Butterworth employs intertextual spectrality as a way of engaging with history, social, economic and political exclusion and the haunted state of contemporary England.

Appropriating and reframing a recognizable literary source, *Jerusalem* is structurally predicated on an intertextual spectrality that creates a new space for audience reaction and engagement. Theatricalizing ideas of influence and inheritance across generations, the intertextual specters in this twenty-first century English drama implicate audiences in the precarious and political process of meaning-making. Creating uncertainty and tension, each spectral moment opens up space for discussions of alternatives, as well as the recognition of visibility and presence. Butterworth argues that 'the first and best trick of the theatre' is 'the tension between what's onstage and what's off'.[21] He proposes that theatre has the capacity to show us 'what we are inclined to ignore', and to map 'what we tend to forget'.[22] As a result, his plays are concerned with things that are 'sometimes ignored, surprised, or forgotten, coming back'[23] and this often takes the form of intertextual hauntings. In *Jerusalem*, Butterworth mobilizes the spectral to show how the past continues to inform the politics of the present moment.

Critics claim that 'Jez Butterworth believes in ghosts.[24] In *Jerusalem* he foregrounds the role of the spectral through the haunting presence of a recognizable intertext to offer new layers of meaning, highlighting the heterogeneous dynamic of his contemporary representations by placing them in a persistent dialogic exchange with identifiable works of the English literary canon. Raising Blake's phantasmal intertext, Butterworth celebrates traces of otherness and questions the perceived autonomy or originality of post-millennial English writings. Restaging the source text as a ghostly haunting in the present, his contemporary drama explicitly locates itself as part of a wider literary tradition, as, across the play, intertextual exchanges raise canonical English texts as sources of creative inspiration and understanding in the contemporary moment.

Notes

1. Holdsworth and Luckhurst, 2013, p. 1.
2. In England, the first years of the twenty-first century were marked by a trend for revivifying plays from the past in the changed context of the new

century. Coupled with a renewed presence of the cultural figure of the specter on stage—from Jeremy Dyson and Andy Nyman's new production *Ghost Stories* at the Duke of Yorks Theatre (2010), and a staging of *Hamlet* at the National Theatre (2010), to new productions *Ghost: The Musical* (2011) at the Manchester Opera House and then at the Piccadilly Theatre, London and the twenty-sixth consecutive year of running for *The Woman In Black* at The Fortune Theatre, London—English theatre entered the new millennium saturated with specters.

3. Sophie Nield, 'Theatre of Screams: On Ghosts and Drama', *The Guardian*, 1 Nov 2010 <https://www.theguardian.com/stage/theatreblog/2010/nov/01/theatre-ghost-drama>
4. Sophie Nield, 'Theatre of Screams: On Ghosts and Drama', *The Guardian*, 1 Nov 2010 <https://www.theguardian.com/stage/theatreblog/2010/nov/01/theatre-ghost-drama>
5. Michael Billington, 'Great Performances' *The Guardian*, 13 April 2015 <https://www.theguardian.com/stage/2015/apr/13/theatre-great-performances-actor-mark-rylance-jerusalem-2009>
6. Jez Butterworth, 'Theater Talk: "Jerusalem" Playwright Jez Butterworth and Tony-winning Best Actor, Mark Rylance', *CunyTV75: Youtube* <https://www.youtube.com/watch?v=ENEoRHLuZ1I>
7. Jez Butterworth quoted in Aida Edemariam, 'The Saturday Interview: Jez Butterworth', *The Guardian*, 14 May 2011 < https://www.theguardian.com/theguardian/2011/may/14/saturday-interview-jez-butterworth>
8. Holdsworth and Luckhurst, 2013, p. 2.
9. Michael Simmons Roberts and Paul Farley, *Edgelands: Journeys Into England's True Wilderness* (London: Vintage, 2012) p. 5.
10. David Ian Rabey, *The Theatre and Films of Jez Butterworth* (London: Bloomsbury Methuen Drama, 2015) p. 111.
11. Jez Butterworth, 'Theater Talk: "Jerusalem" Playwright Jez Butterworth and Tony-winning Best Actor, Mark Rylance', *CunyTV75: Youtube* <https://www.youtube.com/watch?v=ENEoRHLuZ1I>
12. Rabey, 2015, p. 139.
13. Elisabeth Angel-Perez in Rabey, 2015, p. 185.
14. Peter Brooks, *The Empty Space* (Harmondsworth: Penguin, 1968) p. 47.
15. Andrew Marr, 'Evictions, Protests, Unrest: How Jerusalem Saw them Coming', *BBC News*, 24 October 2011 <http://www.bbc.co.uk/news/magazine-15427879>
16. Rabey, 2015, p. 129.
17. Billy Bragg, *The Progressive Patriot* (London: Black Swan, 2007) p. 268.
18. Harpin, 2011, p. 72.

19. Jez Butterworth quoted in Sarah Hemming, 'Jez Butterworth's Play Hits the West End', *Financial Times* 29 January 2010 <http://www.ft.com/cms/s/0/03f4c2da-0c64-11df-a941-00144feabdc0.html>

20. Mary Douglas, *Mary Douglas Collected Works Volume II: Purity and Danger: An Analysis of Concepts of Pollution and Taboo* (London: Routledge, 2003) p. 122.

21. Jez Butterworth, *Mojo and a Filmmaker's Diary* (London: Faber, 1998) p. 147.

22. May quoted in Rabey, 2015, p. 2.

23. May quoted in Rabey, 2015, p. 3.

24. Angel-Perez in Rabey, 2015, p. 185. Butterworth's stage dramas effectively captured the popular imagination of post-millennial theatre-goers, offering them new specters for their age through narratives intertextually grown from the poetry and novels of previous periods. Butterworth wrote his first play as a student in 1992, but it wasn't until his third play *Mojo* premiered at the Royal Court Theatre, London in 1995 that he enjoyed major success, winning the Laurence Olivier, an Evening Standard award and the George Devine award. With his fourth play, *Jerusalem* (2009), Butterworth attained both critical and commercial success, not only in England but across the globe. Conquering the West End and Broadway, with citations on school curricula, and numerous awards leading audience members to camp outside theatres for tickets, *Jerusalem* achieved international acclaim.

CHAPTER 3

'Ghostpitality': Specters of the Self in Zadie Smith's *NW* (2012)

Abstract In Derrida's theory of the spectral, the home is not a safe site, but rather exists as a borderland in which liminal states exist side by side. In Zadie Smith's novel *NW* (2012), spectral dimensions of the homely and the domestic connect the 'haunt' to the compulsion to return to a place, as well as to notions of unconditional hospitality to the spectral 'Other'. Through their connections with the architecture and geography of Smith's North West London, the spectres of her novel critically frame England's capital city as 'simultaneously living and spectral' in a series of problematic encounters that demonstrate the consequences of offering unconditional hospitality to the specter. Beginning with a titular concern with space and place, *NW* goes on to establish an extensive exploration of spectral topographies that are mobilized by its various narratives to explore the agency of the past in the present.

Keywords Hospitality • Home • Novel • Other • Space • Guest • Power • Self • Contemporary • Unconditional • London

While Zadie Smith's first novel *White Teeth* (2000) presented the twentieth century as 'the century of strangers',[1] her fourth novel *NW* (2012) approaches the new millennium as a century defined by encounters with strangers. Reflecting on the process of writing, Smith reveals that

© The Author(s) 2018
K. Shaw, *Hauntology*,
https://doi.org/10.1007/978-3-319-74968-6_4

> I didn't begin with any stories, really. Just this single idea of a girl coming to the door [...] once I had the idea of the girl coming to the door, I started to read around the idea of guests and hosts [...] and there's sort of a long philosophical history to those ideas, and inevitably they ended up being a part of the book, and shaping it. And from "Who gets invited?" I went to "Once you're invited, what kind of hospitality is ideal?"[2]

Across *NW*, visitations by parochial specters function to raise the past in the present, forcing its protagonists to confront questions about their life choices and future trajectories. Through a series of host/visitor interactions in marginal spaces and places—from basement flats to small offices, and roof tops to street corners—the spatial and social politics of Smith's novel conspire to suggest the impossibility of absolute hospitality in the 'Unruly England of the real life' (74).

Offering a range of representations of hospitality and its fraught reality, Smith uses her novel to critically explore anxieties about change and identity emergent in post-millennial England. The guest figures of *NW* are not vulnerable, but assertive, disruptive and uncanny. Protagonists recognize themselves in the specter and are forced to confront social doubling through their role as host. What David Coughlan has elsewhere termed 'ghostpitality'[3]— the welcoming in of the specter—motivates characters to reconfigure relationships between host and guest, the rhetoric of property and possession, presenting the novel as an apposite form in which to debate new paradigms of hospitality for a twenty-first century world. While writing *NW*, Smith drew on Derrida's thoughts on secrecy and society. She reflects that, 'I came across a quote. It's my screen saver now, my little scrap of confidence as I try to write a novel. It is a thought of Derrida's and [it is] very simple: "If a right to a secret is not maintained then we are in a totalitarian space."'[4] Derrida argues that 'literature is a kind of public clandestine—the right to say anything, and thus the right to keep a secret, to not say anything'.[5] Drawing upon Derrida's writings to illuminate contemporary encounters and visitations, Smith's novel critically explores the challenge posed by not only confronting the 'Other', but welcoming them in.

Exposing hospitality as a concept limited by its own internal contradictions, *NW* represents a range of threats from within and without that force protagonist hosts to decide who to welcome, who to exclude, and how to maintain their own internal frameworks and power structures in a shared locale. The implications of hospitality in *NW* centre on the trope of the arrival of a stranger who brings change into the world of the host. From its opening pages, in which Leah invites the spectral double Shar into her home, to Natalie's relationship with the phantomic Nathan Bogle, and Felix's failed attempt to be a good Samaritan to a local stranger, Smith's novel critically re-presents the consequences of contemporary 'ghostpitality'. Made visible through the narrative structure, and problematized by symbolic spectral encounters, host/guest interactions and discourses of difference in *NW* combine to suggest the impossibility of unconditional hospitality in twenty-first century England.

Specters of the Self

Throughout his writings, Derrida repeatedly highlights that 'we do not know what hospitality is', but he does attempt to outline how the dynamics of hospitality can be better understood through the power, space and ethical relations of contemporary social encounters. Building on the earlier work of Benveniste (1973), Levinas (1989) and Kant (2009), Derrida's writings interrogate the host/guest relationship to reveal a paradox that lies at the heart of hospitality. The uncanny aspect of hospitality is evident in the etymological origins of the word—'hospital-ity' being from a Latin root, but derived from two proto-Indo-European words meanings 'stranger', and 'power'.[6] Émile Benveniste traces the roots of the term back to two words: 'Host is', implying reciprocity and equal exchange and 'potis', implying mastery.[7] Hospitality is predicated upon ownership, power, and a stable sense of place. The owner of the home must not only have power in order to host, and they must also have, and maintain, control over the situation. For Derrida, the notion of having and retaining the mastery of the house underlies hospitality; '"Make yourself at home" is an invitation that at once seeks to extend hospitality but also couches this within exacting limits [...] it means: please feel at home, act as if you were at home, but, remember, that is not true, this is not your home but mine, and you are expected to respect my property.'[8] The trope of antecedence is mobilized here to capture the spatial and temporal dimensions of hospitality and the questions of residence and history, past and present, it raises.

Hospitality is also a form of double-gesture, since only with the coming of the stranger can the host identify the power and security of their home and assumed role as receiver:

> He [the host] receives the hospitality that he offers in his own home; he receives it from his own home—which, in the end, does not belong to him. The hôte as host is a guest [...] The one who welcomes is first welcomed in his own home. The one who invites is invited by the one whom he invites.[9]

In this sense, hospitality is also about establishing, maintaining or reinforcing boundaries and divisions. This form of hospitality 'presupposes [...] the possibility of a rigorous delimitation of thresholds or frontiers',[10] of distinctions between inside and outside, the domestic and the public, the self and the Other.

Derrida's distinction between conditional and unconditional hospitality builds on suggestions already evident in the ethics of Lévinas, in proposing a key difference between the 'law' of hospitality and 'laws' of hospitality: 'the law of unlimited hospitality (to give the new arrival all of one's home and oneself, to give him or her one's own, our own, without asking a name, or compensation, [...] and on the other hand, the laws (in the plural), those rights and duties that are always conditioned and conditional'.[11] In his argument, Derrida effectively endorses Lévinas' view that absolute hospitality requires the 'host' to allow 'guests' to behave as they wish. This notion of 'unconditional hospitality' implies that if the guest 'deprives you of your mastery or your home, you have to accept this [...] that is the condition of unconditional hospitality: that you give up the mastery of your space, your home'.[12]

Unconditional hospitality involves relinquishing control and power and instead welcoming the guest without judgement or expectation. In order to demonstrate true hospitality, the host must welcome the visitor in without any preconceived requirements, and in doing so reveals 'the messianic as hospitality, the messianic that introduces deconstructive disruption or madness in the concept of hospitality, the madness of hospitality, even the madness of the concept of hospitality'.[13] If the host engages in 'filtering, choosing' who and what they accept in, they are effectively 'excluding and doing violence',[14] and not acting hospitably. As a result, unconditional hospitality 'presupposes a break with hospitality in the ordinary sense, with conditional hospitality, with the right to or pact of hospitality'.[15]

Hospitality illuminates the paradoxical welcoming of Otherness, the contradictions of opening oneself up to an unknown guest. In practice, 'absolute hospitality requires that I open up my home and that I give not only to the foreigner [...] but to the absolute, unknown, anonymous other, and that I give place to them, that I let them come, that I let them arrive, and take place in the place I offer them, without asking of them either reciprocity (entering into a pact) or even their name'.[16] Problems with these proposed dynamics arise because the act of surrendering all claims to ownership and power also renders it impossible for the individual to function as a host. The unconditional ideal and the necessarily conditional reality of hospitality are inseparable, antinomic and contradictory. Both 'incorporate one another at the moment of excluding one another, they are dissociated at the moment of enveloping one another'.[17] Consequently, the paradox of hospitality is that the condition of its possibility is also the condition of its impossibility.

The relationship between hospitality and hauntology is both complicated and demanding, since a precondition of hospitality involves an acceptance by both the host and the guest that each may change or disturb the other. Indeed, Derrida explores the etymological resonances of hôte and hospitality with 'enemy'[18] and 'hostage',[19] etymological traces that convey a sense of danger and violence in any act of unconditional hospitality. He warns that one consequence of hospitality may be 'the deconstruction of the at-home',[20] and exposure to the unknown and potentially uncontrollable. Controversially, Derrida goes on to assert that 'even if the other deprives you of your mastery or your home, you have to accept this. It is terrible to accept this, but that is the condition of unconditional hospitality: that you give up the mastery of your space, your home, your nation. It is unbearable.'[21] Here, Derrida draws attention to the relationships between identity and relationships and hospitality as a lived experience, and exclusion as a mechanism by which communities can contain or manage the Other.

Welcoming the Other into 'the intimacy of the at home'[22] moves the host from a settled state of domicile and power into transit and trauma, and subjects the stable domestic spaces to disruption and change that generates a sense of 'displacement and unbelonging'.[23] When the home is violated without permission, the presence of the Other can incite moves to protect the home from invasion and a renewed demonstration of mastery over, or ownership of, the newly contested space, as well as a new perspective on the guest as a potentially hostile subject, or worse, a hostage taker. Aligning the guest and the ghost, Derrida recognizes that absolute hospitality is fraught with potential problems: it involves opening the door to a stranger guest 'without horizon of expectation, an opening to the newcomer whoever that may be. It may be terrible because the newcomer may be a good person, or may be the devil.'[24] In extending an invitation, the host must be prepared to welcome invited—but also uninvited—guests into their sphere of influence and ownership. The law of 'unlimited hospitality' in Derrida's writings implies 'that you don't ask the other, the newcomer, the guest to give anything back, or even to identify himself or herself'.[25]

While Smith is not the first author to explore the boundaries and politics of hospitality in contemporary English fiction, her novel does effectively mobilize hospitality as a framework within which to explore questions of loyalty, betrayal and trust. In *NW*, Smith interrogates the consequence of loyalty to a location and the limits of hospitality through a series of temporally distinct visitations and encounters that unsettle and create a new state of uncertainly regarding who is 'visitor', who is 'guest' and where 'home' actually is. In this model of relations, both host and guest share a loyalty to a specific locale that inspires a demonstration of solidarity through the act of unconditional hospitality to the Other, one that carries with it the potential to present a counter to the power and priority of the established host. Reflecting on representations of hospitality in *NW*, Smith claims

> I kind of wanted to make a book in which you had to think about such things on a very basic level. Not, "How do I feel about 20,000 immigrants coming on one day into my country?" but extend hospitality as a result of shared locality, identity, belonging, "How do I feel about a girl at my door?" Fundamentally they're the same questions, but they're reduced to a very local form. That's what interested me [...] I think the anxiety is the same. The idea of what you owe this person who arrives at your door, or what they owe you, and how much they have to be like you in order for you to sympathize with them is, I think, a fundamental question [...] It's easier to make general political principles and large statements, but day by day we're always making these kind of choices: who we let in, who we don't let in, who we approve, who we don't approve within our little circles. What our community is.[26]

In an expression of narrative hospitality, Smith self-consciously structures *NW* around a series of interactions that challenge boundaries between 'who we let in, who we don't let in', between private and public, and in doing so exposes the limits of hospitality in a twenty-first century world.

NW is structured into five sections, each bearing a title that offers a summative account of its various spectral encounters. The opening 'Visitation' of the first section establishes hospitality motivated by shared locality as an overarching theme of the text. The second section, entitled 'Guest', relays a visit by Felix to his father and ex-lover Annie; the third 'Host' is narrated by Natalie in a series of sections numbered 1–185; the fourth 'Crossing' tells the story of Natalie and Nathan's walk across North West London (NW) through directions ('Willesden Lane to Kilburn High

Road'); while the final section 'Visitation' cyclically bring readers back to the opening image of a host/visitor interaction. Challenging established claims of priority and arrival, as well as highlighting the consequences of offering hospitality to the specter, each visitation demands a reconfiguring of space and time, a new consideration of the role of the past in the present, and a reflection on the impossibility of absolute hospitality in twenty-first century England.

LOCAL HAUNTS

If to return to a place is to haunt it, the work of Zadie Smith haunts North West London. De Certeau argues that 'haunted places are the only ones people can live in'[27] and the locale of Smith's *NW* motivates its protagonists to engage in acts of hospitality through a sense of loyalty to, and solidarity with, this cartographically specific space in the city. Smith profiles a North West corner of the capital containing a diversity of districts, from Hampstead and Kentish Town to Willesden and Kilburn that combine to offer the 'NW' postcode of her title. The physical, cultural and social landscapes of this area are a 'regular haunt' of her characters, a space they call home, in which boundaries between the domestic and the public blur, enabling visitation and transgression from a series of visitors. Across the novel, characters move 'From A to B' (38) then 'From A to B redux' (39) in routes defined by repetition and return. Specters materialize in relation to these spatial arrangements and are defined by their geographical situatedness, a sense of place revealing motivations, informing manifestations or relaying communication about each visitation. As spectral places, the haunted space of North West London demands focus on both where specters emerge from and their transformative effects on that site.

Smith was born in North West London, and grew up in the area. The topography of her canon to date draws on these biographical experiences, profiling the suburbs of the capital, rather than its centre. In 'writing obsessively about two miles of town'[28] Smith continues an established English literary tradition. Her representations of contemporary London draw on a literary heritage that can be read back to Charles Dickens and Salman Rushdie in which London is represented in terms of its imperial past and legacies. Focusing on the specific area from Willesden Green, through to Cricklewood and Kilburn, Zadie Smith's North West London is home to a distinct mix of racial communities united by the shared symbols of a postcode, but divided by competing social, economic and cultural forces. Presenting a sharp focus on this common geography but also on the disparate lives, histories and experiences of the individuals contained within this area, Smith's novel maps a range of contemporary social issues onto the changing space of twenty-first century London.

First published in August 2012, following the euphoric summer of the 2012 London Olympics, *NW* offers a very different vision of a city of winners and losers through a claustrophobic concentration on a limited, and limiting, topography. Her novel offers a new imaginary of London as experienced by characters influenced by, but not central to, its city centre. Set in a highly localized and tight-knit London community, *NW* is populated by characters who are almost exclusively born or raised there, and who have failed to stray far from its borders. Thirty years on from her childhood, protagonist Leah still 'passes the old estate every day on her walk to the corner shop' (68) and is 'as faithful in her allegiance to this two-mile square of the city as other people are to their families, or their countries' (5). Geographically, Natalie has moved on a little, to 'the posh bit, by the park' (10) but emotionally, she still lives within eye-sight of her old housing estate. Felix similarly reads the fading memory of his childhood through the familiar topography of Willesden: 'Five and innocent at this bus stop. Fourteen and drunk. Twenty-six and stoned. Twenty-nine and in utter oblivion [...] You live in the same place long enough, you get memory overlap' (117).

Recentring 'the multiverse' (61) of the capital city around the specificities of a single region, *NW* draws attention to marginal spaces and characters. As Felix reflects, 'the tube map [...] did not express his reality. The centre was not "Oxford Circus" but the bright lights of Kilburn High Road' (163). The landscape of Kilburn is socially 'brutal', architecturally defined by modernist 'high-rise towers' and economically 'ungentrified, ungentrifiable. Boom and bust never come here. Here bust is permanent' (47). A world away from the 'little terraces' and 'faux-Tudor piles' that grace Willesden, the novel accentuates the differences within a single area of the North West region of London. In its championing of the local, *NW* offers small-scale change as a marker of broader social, economic and political processes at play in contemporary England. Across the novel, Leah notes wider social and economic shifts in English society through their micro-impact on her local Caldwell/Willesden haunts. There is now an 'organic market [...] in the playground of Leah's old school' because, as she wryly reflects, 'Quinton Primary is a good enough place to buy a croissant but not a good enough place to send your children' (20).

Elsewhere in Caldwell, the 'church of her childhood in which she was a Saturday Brownie, has been converted into luxury apartments, each with its own section of jaunty stained-glass window. Outside, a gathering of sporty little cars parked where once there was a small graveyard' (56). Both 'out of time, and out of place' (77), 'her' school and 'her' church are made uncanny by the intrusion of time into the space of memory. These buildings constitute not only significant memory markers of her heritage and identity, but also function to highlight 'memory overlap' and a sense of change.

As products of this place and time, Smith's characters are both enabled and disabled by the literal and metaphorical boundaries of their locality, comforted by its local vistas and trapped by its socio-economic frameworks. Smith describes England as 'a nation divided by postcodes and accents, schools and last names'.[29] In *NW*, her characters experience the social reality of these contemporary divisions through an acute awareness of geographic boundaries—the estate and the 'nicer' areas, the suburbs and the city—but also less tangible boundaries of class, race and gender that are equally shaped by the power of the postcode. In her cartographically specific representation of this place, Smith suggests that 'postal districts have not only a geographical meaning but a social and economic one as well'.[30] As her novel develops, 'the question of who makes it out of Caldwell and why, as well as the possibility of ever entirely escaping it' comes to dominate the narrative.[31]

In interview, Smith reflected that '*NW* feels like my first novel in some ways, maybe because it's the first I've written as what my mother would call "a grown ass woman"'.[32] Her novel traces the process of becoming 'a grown ass woman' as experienced by two friends—Leah and Natalie—who share the space of North West London and the time of the late twentieth and early twenty-first centuries. As their narratives develop, each is confronted by a specter from the past that inspires an attempted act of ghostpitality in the present which proves to have a transformative effect on their future. Both Leah and Natalie are born and raised in North West London and continue to haunt the area as adults, yet each woman experiences this shared space and time in different ways.

Doubly distanced by her gender, sexuality and education—a university degree is little more than an irritating 'bungee cord, lowering in and pulling out with dangerous velocity' (32) from the Caldwell society of her youth—Leah increasingly views 'time as a relative experience' (33). For Leah, the 'problem seems to be two different conceptions of time. She knew the pull of her animal nature should, by now, be making the deci-sions. Perhaps she's been a city fox for too long [...]. Why won't every-body stay still? She has forced a stillness in herself, but it has not stopped the world from continuing on' (76). The image of 'foxes and what they might symbolise' (52) develops across the narrative, culminating in Leah's realization that in twenty-first century London, 'foxes are everywhere' (307). In a dream-like visitation, her deceased father reports that there is a 'NORTH WEST FOX EPIDEMIC' (51), and likens the life of the fox to that of contemporary Londoners ('that's how we live now, defending our own little patch', 51). The metaphor of Leah as the 'fox' of *NW* extends beyond the physical characteristics of her red hair and Celtic ori-gins to her marginalized position in relation to her specific location. As a 'city fox' Leah becomes acutely adapted to her urban environment and remains devoted to a distinct territorial space within London. Beginning and ending the novel in the basement garden of a council flat, yards away from her place of birth, the narrative wryly reminds us that as a permanent host, 'Leah, born and bred, never goes anywhere' (50).

In *NW*, notions of boundaries and belonging are significant in host/visitor encounters and often frame the reception of the Other into the private space of the host. In its opening pages, Leah experiences an encounter that challenges any stable sense of time and place. Despite her hope that a trip down the 'hallway can only lead to good things' (5), Leah is confronted with a 'stranger' (5) whose visitation marks a 'strange con-vergence' (41) between the public and private worlds of Willesden and of the novel itself. As the narrative reminds us, 'Leah is as faithful in her allegiance to this two-mile square of the city as other people are to their families, or their countries' (6), and consequently 'her guest' (8) is the recipient of absolute hospitality as a direct result of being 'born just there' (12). Extending hospitality and performing the role of 'host' to an 'unex-pected visitor' Leah sacrifices power and domination.[33] The intrusion of the visitor into the peace of Leah's home is signalled by the sound of her doorbell that 'is not being rung. It is being held down' (5). The urgency this implies motivates Leah to speed to the front door and to note through its frosted glass 'a body, blurred. Wrong collection of pixels for it to be Michel' (5). This image is again fractured by the sound of a woman 'screaming PLEASE and crying. A woman thumps the door with her fist' (5). Panicked into submission, Leah opens the door to her visitor who responds with the cryptic cry 'I live here, I live just here, please God—check, please—' (5). Confronted with a counter-claim of control, propriety and power, Leah notes the physical appearance of her visitor and marks out its difference to her own state. The woman standing on her threshold has 'dirty nails', a 'little body' that 'smells' and skin that 'looks papery and dry, with patches of psoriasis on the forehead and on the jaw' (5). Despite these differences, an uncanny aspect is undeniable—'the face is familiar. Leah has seen this face many times in these streets' (5). By way of explanation, her visitor announces that she is 'Shar. My name is Shar. I'm local. I live here' (6). Clouding the space and ownership of Leah's home, Shar's repeated claim to 'live here' breaks down perceived boundaries between public and private space, melding the territory of Caldwell into a fluid realm of shared heritage.

Motivated by 'goodwill' (8) and the fact that both women 'went Brayton!' (9), Leah invites Shar into her home; the two chat about their lives 'in relation to these coordinates [...] they position their own times' (9). As the pair stand in Leah's kitchen drinking tea, 'they look like old friends on a winter's night, holding their mugs with both hands' (12) but gradually their conversation reveals that the two women share little beyond their zone of residence. Shar claims to have supernatural powers, the ability to 'tell things' (11) including the gender of Leah's early stage pregnancy, and as their conversation becomes strained, Leah observes that 'Shar has a dark look. She grins satanically. Around each tooth the gum is black' (11). The power relations of their relationship gradually change across the encounter, and by the time Shar leaves her home it is Leah who performs the role of visitor as she 'follows' Shar, and notes she is 'growing into a new meekness' (13). As a result of the encounter, Leah is left resembling a 'woman in a war zone standing in the rubble of her home' (5).

Shar seeks asylum in Leah's home on fictional grounds—her motivations are economic rather than personal. Leah attempts to extend absolute hospitality based on a shared sense of heritage and location but, in her act of hospitality, Leah enables Shar to reappropriate her home, and dislodge her position of dominance. Welcoming the 'stranger',[34] Leah extends an open invitation into the realm of her power and control and so exposes herself fully to the will of the Other. In most contemporary social experiences of hospitality, the priority and power of the host is absolute, and the guest cannot claim an equal right in, or to the space of, the home. Shar reverses these power relations, taking over the space of Leah's home and its resources. As their encounter develops, Leah and Shar, the 'master and the stranger switch positions, the inviting host becomes the hostage of the guest and thus the guest, the invited hostage, becomes the master of the host […] Because of these substitutions everyone becomes everyone else's hostage'.[35] Shar exposes Leah to a form of reverse colonization, dispossessing her of space and time, disrupting her security and spiralling her established and safe domestic space into a state of flux.

The scam performed by Shar 'is obvious to everyone except Leah' (16) and inspires open hostility in those around her. In contrast to 'the desperate girl who came to the door' (22) Leah recounts, Leah's mother calls Shar 'a Gypsy' (17), while her husband Michel terms Shar 'A crackhead. A thief' (22). For Michel, Leah's actions towards Shar betray hospitality as a weakness. He instead encourages Leah to 'separate yourself from this drama below! This is my point: […] this is what *you* do, perfect example, this girl, *you* let her in' (29). The threat posed by Shar is later aligned to wider pressures, when Leah turns to confront Shar to find 'her face turns into his face and his voice comes out of her throat' (41). Hearing Michel's voice ventriloquized through the Other, Leah is distanced further from the world around her.

It is only when Shar returns to Leah's home in the days that follow and performs the same scripted 'emergency' ('My mum had a heart attack. Five […] pounds', 26) that Leah realizes the girl is 'too far gone to remember her lines' (27) and that she has failed in her attempt to extend absolute hospitality. Shar's performance foregrounds the return that comes to define their relationship. The image of Shar haunts Leah throughout the novel and their 'strange convergence' (41) initiates a form of mid-life crisis. Leah spends the weeks and months that follow the encounter 'On the lookout for her […] Expecting her out of this shop, from behind this corner, by that phone box' (43). The narrative notes that Shar 'is more real to Leah in her absence' (43) yet Leah will 'keep bumping into her' (60) for the duration of the narrative until she comes face to face with photographic images of her visitor mixed into her own printed images. She notes in her pack of prints a photo of 'Shar. Unmistakable' (94), 'a skaggy redhead, skin and bone and track marks, with a fag hanging out her mouth' (95). Michel attempts to reassure Leah that Caldwell is 'a small place' and 'photographs get mixed up' (95) but Leah is nevertheless spooked by the 'insane coincidence' (95) of their spectral encounters.

When Leah opens her door to an anonymous visitor in the opening pages of *NW*, she not only invites her visitor to enter her home, but invites a symbolic crossing of the threshold between outside and inside that the door to the domestic home represents. Like a vampire that needs to be invited into the home of its Gothic host, Leah's visitor comes to symbolize 'that unbearable orb of intimacy that melts into hate.'[36] This fraught relationship between host and guest suggests the impossibility of unconditional hospitality, but also serves to illuminate the pervasive presence of the past in *NW*. The opening visitation of the novel raises unresolved issues relating to identity, space and time, but also illuminates Leah's secrets in the present, making visible the choices she must confront in order to become 'the sole author' (3) of her future. Traumatized by her own failed attempt at absolute hospitality, the unrestricted intrusion of the Other effectively destabilizes Leah's position as host, initiating a series of crises of propriety and power that collectively function to illuminate the lived reality of ghostpitality.

DOUBLE AGENT

In her 2009 essay on writing practice, 'That Crafty Feeling', Smith considers former US President Barack Obama as an example of the politics of 'doubling'. Discussing Barack 'Obama's doubling ways'[37] she outlines his precarious position as a mixed race man in a position of power, one who has necessarily moved away from his original roots, but remains connected through accent and culture. Smith argues that this dual identity means that Obama always inspires 'the sense of a double-dealer, of someone who tailors his speech to fit the audience, who is not of the people (because he is able to look at them objectively) but always above them'.[38] This between-state, a liminal position in which complete belonging to either group is impossible, demands the question 'How can the man who passes culturally between black and white voices with such flexibility, with such ease, be an honest man?'[39] Imagining Obama and other educated mixed race individuals as 'a tragic mulatto, torn between pride and shame'[40], Smith establishes the paradoxical and problematic position, experience and image of doubleness that she goes on to explore in *NW*.

Presenting characters and readers with a physical manifestation of the uncanny—'the return of the repressed ... [of] everything that ought to have remained secret and hidden but has come to light'[41]—the double functions in literature as a canvas for debates about identity, the self and psychology. Noting the prevalence of the double in contemporary novels, Smith has argued that our modern day fascination with doubling is the result of a wider 'indeterminacy [with] a generation obsessed with things which are indeterminate, where you can't be certain of things'.[42] *NW* is concerned with double lives, double standards and representations of doubles, all situated within the context of a profoundly localized space. Smith explores the hidden and outer worlds of her characters to document the politics of concealment and the ongoing interplay of private and public selves. In *NW*, the double functions to betray broader issues relating to the identity of protagonists who mobilize the spectropolitics of their marginal positions as a potential site of change in the present, and agency for the future.

Natalie begins life in *NW* as Keisha Blake, a girl who grows up alongside Leah in similar socio-cultural and economic circumstances. However, as their lives develop, their personal paths diverge and Keisha becomes more ambitious, religious and studious than Leah. By the time she has reached university, Keisha is 'crazy busy with self-invention', and has rebranded herself as Natalie Blake, with a new Westernized identity. In marrying Frank De Angelia, a man 'born on a yacht somewhere in the Caribbean and raised by Ralph Lauren' (204), Natalie synthesizes his social status into her own through a new married name that further distances her from the Keisha Blake of her childhood. Natalie also relocates to a house that is 'twice the size of a Caldwell double' (247) and is physically set apart from the council rented properties where Leah continues to reside. In stark contrast to Leah's small, rented two-bedroom basement flat with its shared garden and dated interior, Natalie's home is a world of 'Security systems. Fences. The carriage of a 4×4 that lets you sit alone above traffic' and, as Natalie reflects, 'she could not help the street on which she was born' (178), yet here movement from Caldwell to a wealthier area of London is, as Leah surmises, 'from there to here, a journey longer than it looks' (12). For Leah, Natalie's home is a physical symbol that money has put 'distance' (252) between her friend and their shared Caldwell origins.

As a young girl, Keisha deeply identifies with literary heroine 'Jane Eyre' (183). Like Jane, Keisha is an intelligent girl who is confronted with inequality and socio-economic disadvantage from an early age. She is an advocate of gender equality and her belief in justice leads to a series of encounters with professional individuals who are inspired to offer her patronage. During their school years at 'Brayton' Leah 'befriended everyone without distinction or boundary' (18) an approach of which 'Keisha Blake had no understanding'. In stark contrast to her friend's 'generosity of spirit', Keisha demonstrates only 'cerebral wilfulness' (18) and a desire to succeed as an individual. The narrative notes that this 'celebrated will and focus did not leave her much time for angst' (185). As such, Keisha is able to transcend the usual tensions and traumas of her teenage years to instead focus on academic prowess and attainment.

Keisha's teenage boyfriend Rodney Banks is a committed Christian who studies with Keisha and shares her ambition and work ethic. Keisha notes his admiration for Machiavelli's *The Prince*, a text he had highlighted so much 'it became one block of yellow and he didn't dare return it to the library' (198). One quote in particular grabs both Rodney and Keisha: 'The difficult situation and the newness of my kingdom force me to do these things, and guard my borders everywhere' (198). Featured in the section of the novel entitled 'Undercover', this quotation succinctly captures the feelings of Rodney and Keisha as interlopers into the middle-class white world of academia. This imposter syndrome stays with Keisha throughout the novel, variously motivating and undermining her attempts to 'reach my full potential' (287). The power of imposter syndrome is outlined to her in explicit terms by Natalie's black female mentor in the legal profession. Herself the victim of discrimination across her acclaimed career, Theodora warns Natalie that, in the legal profession, white male middle-class English judges are accustomed to facing white male middle-class barristers, who function as doubles of themselves. In this reality, Natalie will always be an interloper whose skin and appearance is 'never neutral' (239).

Keisha is also characterized by Shar as a 'Coconut' (9) and, by the time she goes to university, readers are reminded of the 'two sets of accounts Keisha was now in the habit of keeping. On one side of the ledger she placed Rodney, Marcia, her siblings, the church and Jesus Christ himself. On the other, Leah' (199). In a subsection entitled 'Surplus value, schizophrenia, adolescence', Keisha recognizes her childhood friend Layla as real in the mirror, but recognizes herself only as a cheap imitation of the same image (221). Reinterpreting the work of Freud, Lacan argues that the initial perception of an external image of the body produces in the child a response that leads them to establish a conception of 'I' and to become aware of the self. In comparison to the child's own in-formation status, the fully formed body in the mirror image becomes a goal state, an 'Ideal-I' which the child aims to reach as they progress into adulthood. Natalie's encounter with the mirror underlines that her childish ego is dependent on external factors, or 'others', from which she goes on to draw her personality. This Lacanian moment of (mis)recognition deepens Keisha/Natalie's internal divisions and further underpins her fractured sense of self and belonging. In this paradigm of subjectivity, a combination of ego and narcissism direct and inform her growing relationship between self and body.

As she grows older, Natalie realizes that she 'dislikes being reminded of her own inconsistencies' (63), and is 'a person unsuited to self-reflection' (252). Instead, she focuses on maintaining and expanding her collection of conflicting selves, keeping hidden the multiple facets of her personality and identity. As an adult, Natalie constructs an intricate series of narratives that conspire to mask her illicit activities, to maintain her social image as a wife and mother, and to further her career as a high achieving black woman in the legal profession. Natalie's career as a barrister practising commercial law means that by the third section of *NW* she has achieved the role of 'Host'. Having assumed the identity of a middle-class English acceptor of guests, Natalie reaches a point at which she has successfully positioned herself at the centre of power; she is the giver of dinner parties, and the receiver of guests. Her personal mantra—'I am a highly educated black woman. I am a successful lawyer' (273)—articulates the performativity of her outward role, and the narrative she uses to convince herself and others of her performed identity. At work, Natalie 'dressed as a successful lawyer in her early thirties' (263) and repeatedly asserts that she is not a passive 'banker's wife' (273). Speaking to other women in her role as a spokesperson for professional black women, Natalie claims that the secret to her success is 'refusing to set myself artificial limits' (287).

As she grows older, Natalie finds herself confronted not only by the pressures of her race and social class, but also of her gender. She initially becomes aware of the temporal and social expectations of her gender through a visit to her brother. Jayden lives with a group of other men and appears to lead a carefree life, partying in local gay nightclubs including the famous Vauxhall Tavern. Sitting in his apartment, exhausted after a day at work, and in the midst of her brother's seemingly carefree world, Natalie notes with amazement that this male 'arrangement was timeless—it did not come bound by the constructions of time—and this in turn was the consequence of a crucial detail: no women were included within the schema. Women come bearing time. Natalie had brought time into this house. She couldn't stop mentioning the time, and worrying about it' (264). Bound by the constraints of time—the time to go to work or go home, or the time to settle down and have a baby—Natalie functions as both a gendered double of her brother and a reminder of the gendered expectations of time on female experience. As section 166 of her narrative notes, with each year that passes 'Time Speeds Up', and her experience of time also quickens with age. Reflecting on the racing pace of her thirties, Natalie claims that she 'had been eight for a hundred years. She was thirty-four for seven minutes' (275).

The reality of life as a working mother is exposed by her narrative as a collective lie in which many women—including Natalie herself—are complicit. Despite acting out the image of a high achieving woman balancing children and work, Natalie knows that 'each time she returned to work the challenge was perfectly clear: make it happen so it seems like it never happened. There was much written about this phenomenon in the "Woman" section of the Sunday supplements [...]. The key to it all was the management of time' (274). Natalie is cold and aloof when her employee Melanie tearfully confesses to missing her small child and struggling as a working mother, detachedly reflecting on her position as a 'grand seigneur to whom a frightened peasant had come, with a confession about the harvest' (266). Setting the double image of working mother against the reality of an inflexible and intolerant workplace environment, Natalie's narrative exposes the difficulties encountered by working mothers in contemporary English society. Trapped between, and dually committed to, work and childbearing, Natalie is placed under increasing social, economic and political pressure which she attempts to escape via a range of alternative 'selves'.

Natalie negotiates these constraints by living her life as a form of '*Conspiracy*' (236). As her numerically sectioned narrative pointedly notes, 'Blake was a double agent' (268). Through the performativity of self-doubling, Natalie operates as a 'double agent', creating alter-egos through which her most secret desires can be indulged and explored. Natalie's computer screen literalizes this split-identity, masking her alternative sexual life with her role as a mother, as 'hidden behind the image of Spike was another window, of listings', 271). Through her online alter-ego Natalie is able to experience being a visitor to the homes of anonymous swingers under her assumed online indentity. Yet she rarely receives hospitality or satisfaction from her hosts and despite her best efforts, her alternative identities remain difficult to negotiate and maintain.

Eventually 'Natalie's storytelling' (242) and dual life as a 'Cava socialist' (247) are exposed. Section 170 of her story is pointedly entitled '*In drag*' (245), a summation of her approach to the numerous roles she adopts as a black woman in contemporary society. Performing an increasingly diverse dramatic personae of characters, Natalie acts out 'Daughter drag. Sister drag. Mother drag. Wife drag. Court drag. Rich drag. Poor

drag. British drag. Jamaican drag. Each required a different wardrobe'
(278). Each role enables Natalie to live out a different aspect of her personality, but the pressure of trying to maintain some and conceal other
roles leads to Natalie being exposed. When Frank stumbles across Natalie's
emails he discovers her secret online identity—'KeishaNW@Gmail.com'
(294)—an identity constructed using her childhood name and childhood
geography, and one that explicitly situates her within, rather than between,
social class boundaries. Interpreted by her husband as an explicit rejection
of her married name and identity, this moniker motivates Frank to question the 'fiction' (294) of their relationship and her authenticity. His
wounded demand 'Who *are* you?' (295) leads to her ejection her from the
family home and her role as host, back onto the streets as a guest in North
West London.

When Natalie walks out of the family home she realizes that she is head-
ing towards another, existentialist 'NW'—'Nowhere' (295). As she walks,
she emits 'a queer keening noise, like a fox' (299), a description that
echoes the 'city fox' Leah in their shared territory of Caldwell and
Willesden. Natalie flees her family home wearing 'a big T-shirt, leggings
and a pair of filthy red slippers' and only once she is on the streets of North
West London does she realize that she looks 'like a junkie' (299), a cold
and lost double of Shar, wandering the streets without purpose. As she
wanders, Natalie attempts to absolve herself of any sense of self, to achieve
a state in which 'She was no one [...] Walking was what she did now, walking was what she was [...] She had no name, no biography, and no characteristics' (300). Like a trapped animal, Natalie paces the route of her
'NW' until she comes to 'Caldwell's boundary wall' (300). Reaching this
divider between the known and unknown, Natalie walks like a trapped
animal 'along the wall from one end to the other and back again. She
seemed to be seeking some sign of perforation in the brick. She kept
retracing the same area' (300).

At this point Natalie is confronted with a spectral encounter in the form
of her childhood crush, Nathan Bogle. As the narrative wryly notes,
'Nathan Bogle is a person of interest' (332), not only to the police in their
pursuit of Felix's killer, but also because of his spectral relationship to
Natalie Blake. The word 'Bogle' has its origins as a sixteenth century term
for a specter, phantom or bogeyman, a mythical being prone to targeting
people outside their homes at night. Nathan's surname echoes this ghostly
shadow, disrupting the narrative with a haunting apparition of another
aspect of Natalie's identity. The pair share the same initials, childhood

experiences and both find themselves on the run from the consequences of their controversial actions at the end of *NW*. As a young girl growing up, Natalie 'had a crush on Nathan Bogle' (264) and this connection to her past becomes a motivating influence in her walk with him across the shared vistas of their childhoods. In an attempt to diffuse their awkward social encounter as adults, Nathan playfully asks Natalie 'You trying to break back in?' (300) and so draws attention to the presence of her past that his spectral visitation raises.

Like a Dickensian ghost of Christmas past, Nathan Bogle creates a moment of 'sudden and total rupture' (282) with Natalie's present, physically drawing her back into the forgotten streets and spaces of her childhood as 'Keisha'. As a spectral double, Nathan Bogle points out 'I ain't in your dreams, Keisha. You're in mine [...]. You remember me. You know who I am' (316). Their walk traces both the boundary wall of her community and the boundaries of her past and present, physically mapping out the invisible boundaries of class, gender and race that divide not only North West London, but contemporary England. A world away from the middle class suburbs of her former life, the geography of Natalie's walk returns her to a childhood geography of Willesden, encouraging her to re-engage with the community of her youth and recognize how her individualism has distanced her from a stable sense of place and belonging. The geographical specificities of the route betray a deep familiarity with, and fondness for, the streets and roads of Smith's own North West London. Natalie's tour of the areas of her youth make them freshly uncanny, as the final section of the novel and the final walk offer both a literal and metaphorical 'Crossing'.

Only by recognizing and welcoming the specter, walking with it and listening to it, does Natalie finally achieve a more stable sense of self. Although she ends the novel separated from her husband, and their marital conflicts remain unresolved, Natalie does achieve a new sense of her own identity through her gesture of conditional hospitality to Nathan. Identifying the point at which she 'began to exist for other people' (179), Natalie's re-engagement with the spaces and times of her youth encourages her to realize that 'she was still an NW girl at heart' (218). Through a series of rhetorical questions she challenges the relationship between space and time to which she had formerly subscribed, and instead proposes a new dynamic that is informed by her core principles of freedom and choice: 'Whoever said these were fixed coordinates to which she had to be forever faithful? How could she play them false? Freedom was absolute and everywhere, constantly moving location. You couldn't hope to find it only in the old, familiar places' (329). The realization that the life she spent thirty years establishing does not ultimately fulfil her needs leads Natalie to acknowledge 'a connection between boredom and the desire for chaos. Despite many disguises and bluffs perhaps she had never stopped wanting chaos' (304). Re-engaging with the landscape of her past through the spectral encounter with her own personal Bogle, Natalie realizes that she faces 'a choice of either stasis or propulsion' (324)—to live the life of 'Leah lying in the garden in the hammock, totally exposed' (330) to the elements, or to take control and direct the next chapter of her life, ironically, as 'The sole author' (221).

Visitation (Redux)

In interview, Smith has argued that 'we make our own lives [...] you want people to have equality of aspiration and of opportunity, but it doesn't mean that they're going to end up in the same place'.[43] At the end of *NW*, her protagonists have moved less than a few streets from where they were born. Bound to the paradox of their locality and identities, Leah, Natalie and Felix 'can't go home, can't leave home'[44] and so seek new experiences of space and time away from any panoptical view of society through a series of encounters with specters from their past. The existential uncertainty and socio-economic inequality that define Smith's contemporary England means that none of her characters end the novel as the sole authors of their own lives. Using compass direction as a titular and narrative device, the clear geographical landscapes of her novel contrast sharply with a cast of characters who are comparatively directionless, moving forward with their lives, but ultimately ending up back where they started.

Across *NW*, protagonist hosts negotiate visitors as a way of confronting the Other, but these spectral visitations also conspire to expose unconditional hospitality as a potentially daunting and dangerous reality in twenty-first century English society. As Derrida warns, when hosts invite the Other inside unconditionally, they demonstrate extreme optimism, 'because the newcomer may be a good person, or may be the devil'.[45] In *NW*, the potential pitfalls of the ethical idea of demonstrating unconditional hospitality to the Other are made evident through encounters between protagonists and specters. Only through Natalie's encounter with Nathan does the novel offer a paradigm of conditional hospitality that is viable for both host and visitor. Like Leah's efforts to welcome in

Shar, Felix attempts unconditional hospitality but finds that his gesture is futile and self-destructive.[46] These experiences combine to suggest that the 'possibility of hospitality is sustained by its impossibility',[47] as various attempts to engage in acts of unconditional hospitality to the visitor ultimately prove damaging to the host. Through the hospitable encounter, structural repetition and social doubling, Smith critically (re)presents the problematic reality of ghostpitality in the twenty-first century English novel.

NOTES

1. Zadie Smith, *White Teeth* (London: Hamish Hamilton, 2000) p. 281.
2. Zadie Smith quoted in John Self, 'Zadie Smith Interview', *Asylum* <https://theasylum.wordpress.com/2012/09/12/zadie-smith-interview/>
3. David Coughlan, *Ghost Writing in Contemporary American Fiction* (London: Palgrave, 2016) p. 19.
4. Zadie Smith, 'That Crafty Feeling' in *Changing My Mind Essays* (London: Penguin, 2009) pp. 99–110; p. 102.
5. Jacques Derrida, *A Taste for the Secret* (ed.) Maurizio Ferraris (London: Wiley, 2001) p. 53.
6. Kevin D. O'Gorman 'Modern Hospitality: Lessons from the Past', *Journal of Hospitality and Tourism Management* 12 (2) 2005, pp. 141–151; p. 148.
7. Émile Benveniste quoted in Jacques Derrida, *Of Hospitality: Anne Dufourmantelle Invites Jacques Derrida to Respond* (Stanford: Stanford University Press 2000) pp. 71–83; pp. 77.
8. J.D. Caputo, *Deconstruction in a Nutshell: A Conversation with Jacques Derrida* (New York: Fordham University Press 2002) p. 111.
9. Jacques Derrida, *Adieu to Emmanuel Levinas* (trans.) Michael Naas (London: Stanford University Press, 1999) p. 42.
10. Derrida, 2000, pp. 47–49.
11. Derrida, 2000, p. 77.
12. Derrida, 2000, p. 71.
13. Derrida, 2000, p. 50.
14. Derrida, 2000, p. 55.
15. Derrida, 2000, p. 25.
16. Derrida, 2000, p. 25.
17. Derrida, 2000, p. 81.
18. Derrida, 2000, p. 43.
19. Derrida, 2000, p. 76.
20. Derrida, 2000, p. 64.
21. Derrida, 2000, p. 71.

22. Derrida, 1999, p. 28.
23. Derrida, 2000, p. 62.
24. Derrida, 2000, p. 65.
25. Derrida, 2000, p. 71.
26. Zadie Smith quoted in Thomas Page McBee, 'The Rumpus Interview with Zadie Smith', *The Rumpus*, 1 January 2013 <http://therumpus.net/2013/01/the-rumpus-interview-with-zadie-smith/>
27. Michael De Certeau, *The Practice of Everyday Life* (trans.) Steven Rendall (Berkley, LA: University of California Press, 1984) p. 108.
28. Zadie Smith quoted in Christopher Bollen, "Interview: Zadie Smith', *Interview Magazine* <http://www.interviewmagazine.com/culture/zadie-smith/print/>
29. Zadie Smith, 'Dead Man Laughing', *The New Yorker*, 22 December 2008 <http://www.newyorker.com/magazine/2008/12/22/dead-man-laughing>
30. Zadie Smith quoted in Theodore Dalrymple, 'Zadie Smith's London', *City Journal*, Winter 2013 <http://www.city-journal.org/html/zadie-smith%E2%80%99s-london-13541.html>
31. Zadie Smith quoted in Laura Miller, '"NW": Zadie Smith's Neighborhood', *Salon*, 27 August 2012 <http://www.salon.com/2012/08/26/nw_zadie_smiths_neighborhood/>
32. Zadie Smith quoted in John Sclf, 'Zadie Smith Interview', *Asylum* <https://theasylum.wordpress.com/2012/09/12/zadie-smith-interview/>
33. Derrida, 2000, p. 83.
34. Derrida, 2000, p. 71.
35. Derrida, 2000, p. 81.
36. Derrida, 2000, p. 4.
37. Smith, 2009, p. 140.
38. Smith, 2009, p. 140.
39. Smith, 2009, p. 141.
40. Smith, 2009, p. 142.
41. Sigmund Freud, 'The Uncanny', *The Standard Edition of the Complete Psychological Works of Sigmund Freud* (trans.) James Strachey and Anna Freud (London: Hogarth, 1986) pp. 218–252; p. 225.
42. Susheila Nasta (ed.) *Writing across Worlds: Contemporary Writers Talk* (London: Routledge, 2004) pp. 266–278; p. 273.
43. Zadie Smith quoted in Christopher Bollen, "Interview: Zadie Smith', *Interview Magazine* <http://www.interviewmagazine.com/culture/zadie-smith/print/>
44. Zadie Smith, 'Dead Man Laughing', *The New Yorker*, 22 December 2008 <http://www.newyorker.com/magazine/2008/12/22/dead-man-laughing>

45. Derrida, 2000, p. 80.
46. When his absent mother suddenly reappears after eight years without contact, 'Felix took her in' (164) despite the advice of his other family and friends. His reward for this act of hospitality is made apparent the following day when he wakes in his home to find 'she was gone, with Felix's cashpoint card, his watch, all his chains' (165). This failed gesture to invite in the Other is repeated later in his narrative when he rises to offer a pregnant woman a seat on a crowded tube train. His gesture, 'Take mine' (166), does not lead to reward, but to death, as the same men take offence, follow Felix off the Tube at the next stop and stab him in the darkness of a nearby street.
47. Jacques Derrida quoted in Caputo, 2002, p. 111.

CHAPTER 4

Authorial Afterlives: Ghost-writing in David Peace's *PATIENT X* (2018)

Abstract This chapter considers how the capacity of the specter as a double suggests unresolved terms in David Peace's *Patient X* (2018). Doubling is etymologically connected to the spectral and the uncanniness of the specter can alert the living to its pervading presence in their contemporary world. The dynamic of this relationship forms a central concern of Peace's short story cycle. In each story, spectral effects impact on notions of the self, challenging the singular 'I' and raising the possibility of an/other. Through a subtle noise, movement, interactive vision or tactile encounter, the textual presentation of the specter generates questions regarding identity and existentialism in Peace's protagonist. Across the text, the spectral takes many forms, functioning to highlight the unexpected nature of the return, and to raise questions about the self and the Other, the individual and society, and understandings of our historical situatedness.

Keywords Akutagawa • David Peace • Short story • Double • Ghost • Rewriting • Hauntology • Doppleganger

In his 2018 text *Patient X* (2018), David Peace creates a 'haunting paean'[1] of praise for the life and work of Japanese short story writer Ryūnosuke Akutagawa. Peace's 'ghost-writing' operates on the levels of both content and form, rewriting not only the life of another literary author, but doing so through a literary retelling of that author's canonical works. Peace deploys ghost-writing as a technique to engage with a range of social, political and psychological issues that are as pressing in twenty-first century England as they were in early twentieth century Japan. Exploring the potential of spectrality as a subversive and creative textual intervention, Peace's rewritings operate as both under-writings that support and replicate the narrative style and structure of Akutagawa's earlier tales, and as rupture-writings that rewrite Akutagawa's narrative content and representations for a new purpose, and in a new period.

Patient X is an implicitly hauntological project, a collection occupied not only by the extra-textual presence of author Ryūnosuke Akutagawa, but also by the spectral raising of his writings. The title of the collection immediately implies a disconnect—between time and space, being and non-being—through its intense focus on a specific subject that is no longer here. Disrupting the boundaries between writer and reader, originality and origin, the structure of the collection also incites an anticipation of a series of repetitions—'After/Before'—that collapse established notions of temporality. In twelve separate yet inter-connected tales, Peace raises the ghost of Akutagawa as his protagonist to confront the traumas of modernity through repetitive patterns of entrapment and deception and places him in a series of increasingly hostile environments.[2] Mobilizing repetition as an uncanny trope, Peace employs the double to evoke complicity, paranoia and fear as a mode of literary haunting. In fictional terrains dominated by copies, replicas and simulacra, a sonic hauntology is augmented by techniques of repetition and refrain, and by the structural motif of doubling, to illuminate critical connections between the early twentieth century life of Akutagawa and his twenty-first century afterlife in the hands of David Peace.

THE LIFE AND DEATH OF THE AUTHOR

Until the publication of *Patient X*, David Peace was best known for his work as a novelist. However, in the period before writing *Patient X*, Peace spoke publicly about his increasing dissatisfaction with the novel form as a vehicle for fiction. He reflected that 'the novel as a form' had 'begun to depress me',[3] and that novels were no longer 'stimulating people and reflecting the times'.[4] As a writer of fiction in the post-millennial period, Peace argues that it is no longer possible to 'believe in the novel form. Storytelling is already quite ruined by the individualism of Western society

[...] short stories are the only collective experience we have left.'[5] Consequently, his 2018 text maintains many of Peace's characteristic approaches to lyrical prose, but rejects the novel form in favour of the condensed framework and intense focus offered by the short story. Peace reflects that 'ideally, I'd like *Patient X* to be thought of along the lines of an Italian "romanzo di raconti"—a novel of tales—pretentious, I know, and not a form familiar to us. But I don't feel [the] "short story cycle" description is wrong, and it is probably the term we have closest to what I was hoping to achieve'.[6]

Author and critic Frank O'Connor reflects that 'the short story seems to thrive best in a fragmented society'[7] and in the hands of Akutagawa and Peace the form is deployed to capture lived experiences of fragmentation. In an era of fast communication and social change, the short story also offers a sympathetic form for representing contemporary time. Peace's collection of short stories structurally undermine temporal linearity as a result of their micro- and macro-level narrative dynamics. Designed to be read in a particular order, and building upon one another to reveal something larger than the sum of their individual parts, the short story cycle *Patient X* offers an overarching narrative that is used to highlight the disunity inherent to contemporary experience. Through a range of unifying features—including a clear sense of place and a distinct historical era—an underlying pattern of coherence explores an inescapably critical construction. This organic development creates bonds between the twelve short stories that comprise the collection, as well as characteristic elements within each.

The challenge of a writer (re)presenting the life of another writer in his preferred literary mode is significant, and Peace tackles the task motivated by a respect and admiration for the work of his predecessor. In *Patient X*, Peace rewrites both the life and works of Ryūnosuke Akushagawa. The politics of this project began in 1994 when Peace arrived in Tokyo. Without access to the internet, and with limited language skills, he chanced across a translation of *Rashonmon* in a small book shop. Following this, he recalls that 'Akugatawa quickly became my obsession'.[8] Peace wrote the second volume of his Tokyo Trilogy, *Occupied City,* using the same multi-perspective narratorial technique made famous by Akutagawa's *Rashomon*, and cites the author as a 'direct inspiration on my work'.[9] Ryūnosuke Akutagawa wrote in the Taisho period (30 July 1912–25 December 1926), and is popularly regarded as the father of the Japanese short story. To this day the Akutagawa Prize remains the highest literary award in

Japanese culture. Akutagawa wrote more than 150 short stories in his lifetime and was one of the first Japanese modernists to be translated into English. The carefully plotted historical retellings of his early works developed into more emotional and contemporary settings in his later writings, profiling his rare ability to describe sensations and vivid experiences through poetic representations of the everyday.

During his schooling in Japan, Akutagawa developed a wide 'knowledge of literature, particularly of European literature, [that] continued to grow constantly wider and deeper. He read Balzac, Tolstoy, Verlaine, the Brothers Goncourt, Flaubert'.[10] In his writings, Akutagawa aimed to bring together Eastern and Western literature, cultural approaches and practices. Akutagawa wrote his work in a period during which Japanese cultural identity was exposed to Western influences, and to post-war globalizing forces. As a result, his stories reflect the influence of a wider variety of literature from East and West, borrowing from international structures, themes and techniques to represent his own ideas. Recycling works from a diverse range of styles, cultures and periods, his short stories reframe tales from ancient Japan and China with a modern perspective, creating new texts from existing resources. According to Beongcheon Yu 'at least sixty-two of Akutagawa's stories reveal a varying degree of indebtedness to his known literary sources, Japanese, Chinese, Indian and Western'.[11] The short story form enabled him to 'give his perceptions such exquisite and durable form',[12] one that united Japanese tradition and Western cultural influences, to produce unsettling effects and profound questions about the nature of reality and contemporary experience. Akutagawa's short stories offer a rare representation of the impact of modernity on Japan, and the impact of the widespread changes experienced by Japanese society in a relatively short period of time. Peace reflects that Akutagawa offers such insight because 'he lived a dramatic period of Japanese history: earthquakes, a fast modernization, imperialism, war at the gates. His stories were reminiscent of ancient Japanese legends, but it was terribly modern in style and in the interpretation of reality.'[13]

Akutagawa's early access to a wide range of international texts not only informed his global taste for literature, but also encouraged him to develop a penchant for the supernatural. G.H. Healey, a critic of modern Japanese literature, recalls that Akutagawa was always interested in 'tales of ghosts' and, immersing himself in written and oral tales of hauntings, he grew to believe 'somewhere between dream and reality [that] he saw ghosts himself'.[14] By the time Akutagawa reached university 'his interest in the weird and the supernatural had grown, if anything, stronger' and from 1912 onwards 'he began to keep a notebook in which he recorded ghost stories that he collected from friends and relatives or came across in books'.[15] He graduated with a degree in English Literature and taught briefly before becoming a full-time writer. Throughout his career as a writer Akutagawa 'restricted himself almost exclusively to the short story'.[16] These stories fall into two categories—*rekishimono* (historical) and *yasukichimono* (autobiographical)—the former in the early period of his life, and the latter emerging as he approached the final decade before his death.

Akutagawa was 'brilliant' and 'sensitive' but also 'cynical' and 'neurotic',[17] traits captured in the pronounced detachment characteristic of his later works. In one of several suicide notes, he claimed to be motivated by 'a vague unease about my future',[18] while in other letters he reflected on his 'sense of the fundamental evilness of human life and in particular of his resentment of his own fate'.[19] Unlike his earlier historical tales, the stories written in Akutagawa's later years are 'introspective, neurotic, and remarkably depressive'.[20] Thematically, these later works are united by a concern with the dark side of humanity, offering satires on the human condition and representing the bleak undercurrents of the human mind. G.H. Healey reflects that Akutagawa's later writing 'sprang from his pessimistic view of human life. He had come to regard life as a shabby and despicable affair that could only achieve any sort of beauty when refined and polished by art.'[21] In his final years, Akutagawa suffered an 'over sensitivity to imagined humiliations' and an 'extreme depression'[22] that left him 'nervous and easily frightened' and finally 'overcome by attacks'.[23] He eventually committed suicide using an overdose of barbiturates, a sleeping aid, at the age of 35.

In *Patient X*, Peace rewrites Akutagawa's life through short stories that are themselves rewrites of narratives already told across a range of different periods and cultures throughout history. Each of Peace's twelve short stories focus on a single event or effect to open up a plurality of alternative perspectives. Recasting past events, the haunting practice of Peace's ghost-writing is not passive or unoriginal, but an active gesture to re-create and add new layers to Akutagawa's tales. Thematizing the past in the present, and the 'Other' in the self, the transgression of his rewriting captures both the paradoxical realization of uncanniness and the liminal spaces of history, locality and identity. This re-contextualization is used to highlight the relevance of older narratives, as well as the various ways in which the influence of the past can be made manifest in the contemporary period, through the agency of the return. In this double gesture of rewriting, Peace offers alternative ways of reading in the contemporary period, enabling the renegotiation and repositioning of perspectives on earlier texts, and the reassertion of the life of the author, even in the face of his own death.

Peace presents the life and death of the author—in this case Ryūnosuke Akutagawa—as a necessary precondition of his own twenty-first century rewriting. If meaning is not to be found in the origin (author) but in the destination (reader) then in the words of Barthes, 'the birth of the reader must be at the cost of the death of the author'.[24] Releasing Akutagawa's original tales from their author and liberating them as active material to be reshaped and 'read' afresh, the death of the author is offered by Peace as not only the birth of the reader, but also the birth of himself as rewriter. Liberating texts from the interpretative restriction of authorship, Peace's new short stories signal the returning influence and relevance of both Akutagawa and his texts and, in doing so, highlight the agency of rewriting as a political textual intervention in the twenty-first century.

Peace's rewriting of Akutagawa's short stories reanimate Akutagawa as their protagonist Akutagawa, who walks the streets of Japan like a ghost, a man half alive, half dead, and increasingly detached from the world and events around him. Each of the twelve stories in Peace's cycle charts the movement of Akutagawa as he passes through key phases and historical moments in modern Japan. In each situation, Akutagawa is haunted by disturbing visions, chased by his double, or deafened by the noise of machinery as a metaphorical emblem of insanity. *Patient X* opens and closes with short stories that critically consider the death of an author. The tenth tale 'Saint Kappa'[25] uses 'La Mort d'un Auteur' (217) to offer a metafictional parody of Barthes' 'death of the author' to frame rewriting as a creative and critical intervention with political and social motivations and consequences for both author and reader. The introductory note to the story explains that the narrator finds a story in a book shop in Tokyo by the author Yasukichi Horikawa but has been 'unable to find any record of the author, other than his story' (216). It comes with a warning that the story is '*based on* [...] *a retelling by my esteemed contemporary Mr Ryūnosuke Akutagawa. And so I make no claims for the originality of the following words*' (217). Through this formal acknowledgement of the '*preceding and vastly superior masterpieces upon which I have based my own shabby, sorry story*' (217), the fictional narrator tells the tale of another writer and ends with a vision of the writer being cast into the pits of hell, an intertextual reference that literally signals the death of the author and draws the collection full circle to the opening tale, 'After the Thread, Before the Thread' (1).

Patient X begins with a rewriting of a story that has been subject to numerous re-tellings and oral traditions across Eastern and Western cultures.[26] Peace's rewriting takes the imagery and parable-like quality of the original tale and mobilizes its oral tradition and tone of moral instruction to consider the death of the author, Ryūnosuke Akutagawa. In Peace's new story 'After the Thread, Before the Thread', it is not Kandata but Ryūnosuke 'who was writhing in Hell' (3). When offered the chance to escape on the spider's thread he begins to climb it alone. Yet the realization that 'his sins would always follow him, always catch up with him' (6) ultimately leads Ryūnosuke to 'let go of the spider thread' and 'at that very instant, at that very moment, as Ryūnosuke fell back down into the darkest depths, the spider thread broke at the very place where he had been hanging from it' (6). Peace adapts the first story of his collection using the old tale of 'The Spider's Thread' but removes other characters from the literal and metaphorical central thread to allow for a singular focus on his protagonist. He reflects that 'In Akutagawa's version, he falls because the others follow and the thread breaks when others want to follow him. In mine, the others are not there. It is a self-destructive act. He decides to just let go. We have a chance at redemption like him, but we have to sacrifice ourselves, to struggle. We have to say no, I will not be a compulsive consumer, I do not want to be deconstructed, I will not be alone. That's our spider's thread.'[27]

Unlike the rest of the stories in *Patient X*, the opening tale is not period-specific and its temporal framework enables Peace to draw upon the wide range of Western and European literatures and Buddhist spirituality that informed Akutagawa's education. Peace adds Christ to the spiritual landscape of Akutagawa's Buddha in Paradise, because the Japanese author 'was interested in Christianity and was torn apart by trying to reconcile the East and the West, the religions of the East and West and the politics of the East and the West'.[28] Employing repetition as a form of literary exorcism, the story offers an image of the decay of humanity. The quotation from Virgil that ends the tale—'*In girum imus nocte et consumimur igni*' (6)—describes the fate of humanity as cursed to 'go round and round in the night consumed by fire'. The quote is a palindrome, it reads the same backwards and forwards, suggesting that there is neither a start nor an end point to narrative, and that the act of rewriting is an ongoing process in the wider pursuit of understanding the past.

Peace is freed by the death of an author (Akutagawa) in the first short story of *Patient X*, and thereby enabled to conduct a rewriting of both the author's life and work. Suspending the influence of the author creates a new form of subject agency, foregrounding traces of Akutagawa's life and literature that *Patient X* knowingly places and displaces across its short story cycle. Peace's ghost-writing dramatizes the spectrality of the past that returns to haunt the present in the form of the rewrite, returning agency to old works and former lives by offering new representations and models of authorship. Injecting new social, political and economic issues into the context of the original text, Peace's rewriting of Akutagawa's life through his textual occupation of his short stories enables a critical re-visioning, challenging boundaries between the self and Other, and generating a new creative space for transgressive rewritings of author, text and context.

'Everyone Is a Ghost Now'

Repetition is a key feature in the canon of David Peace, and in *Patient X* the author continues this stylistic idiosyncrasy to represent the agency inherent in the act of the return. Peace argues that 'the subject matter has to suggest the style'[29] and although 'you have to reinvent with every book',[30] his persistent employment of dense repetition in this short story cycle functions as a conscious effort to capture the experience of the final period in Akutagawa's life. In a series of stories that highlight the significance of the past to the present, repetition is used to warn against the dangers of forgetting and to help characters to hold on to a precarious grasp of reality. Through an economy of expression, repetition also adds to the pace of the narrative, encouraging readers to race through events and encounters. Peace argues that repetition 'works for me on two levels: every day we do the same things and we say the same things and there is very little variation [...] people live quite repetitious lives. Fiction never seems to pick up on this. I want the books to be realistic.'[31] As his characters make the same mistakes, reprise the same routines and turn over the same problems, repetition becomes an effective means of reflecting on the internal rhythms of early twentieth century Japanese society.

Peace describes the process of constructing *Patient X* as a 'continuous work of rewriting, where even the pure sound and simple word has an essential role. I work here and elsewhere in the things I do on three levels simultaneously: the literal meaning of the words that convey the sound and even the look and feel, as you have spatially the letters on the page.'[32] Drawing on the necessarily repetitive nature of rewriting, this acute awareness transforms *Patient X* into a series of repeated and revisited spectacles that draw attention to their own spectral status. Making visible the hidden elements of both the individual and society, Peace's twelve short stories integrate a sonic hauntology of noises from the past that are repeated in present space. In this conflicting temporality, repetitious occurrences and physical doubling function to re-present both past and present imaginaries through a profoundly haunted time-space. Raising questions of origins and reality, this approach makes the present waver and incites doubt in the protagonist.

Across the twelve connected short stories, protagonist Akutagawa is subject to a repetitive sonic hauntology of menacing sounds and alien signals. Gradually consumed by this hostile auditory landscape, he complains of 'turning gears' (198) that '*block out half my field of vision*' (240) and notes the noise of '*beating of wings*' (241) that force him to 'put his fingers in his ears' (198). Akutagawa is also haunted by visual repetitions, especially the pervading presence of people wearing raincoats that appear similar to his own, a frequent observation that he labels a 'coincidence' (80), yet sends 'a shiver down his spine' (285). These recurring encounters conspire to undermine his confidence and judgement, leading Akutagawa to doubt everything and instead to assume '*anything and everything is a lie. Politics, business, science, art; it's all just a mottled layer of enamel covering over this life in all its horror*' (248). As the story cycle develops, this technique of repetition is taken to a breaking point of cyclical incantation and haunting surveillance.

Derrida argues that the specter is '*always [...] looking at me*'[33] and suggests that the living are 'under surveillance by the specter'.[34] He terms this sensation of being watched the '"visor effect": a sense that the ghost looks at or watches us. Even when it is not materially apparent, the specter is looking, although through a helmet; it is watching, observing, staring at the spectators and the blind seers, but you do not see it seeing, it remains invulnerable beneath its visored armor.'[35] Across the short stories in *Patient X*, Akutagawa articulates his experience of this 'visor effect' and describes experiencing a '*relentless gaze on my back*' (242). Noting the '*crowds now absent, only shadows now present*' (97), Akutagawa becomes increasingly paranoid. As the short stories unfold, he documents a heightened awareness of being watched in both his public and private worlds.

Peace's representation of Ryūnosuke Akutagawa as both the subject and object of the 'visor effect' reaches a pinnacle in the ninth short story of the cycle, 'After the Disaster, Before the Disaster'. The story is set 'after the disaster' of the 1923 earthquake and explores the greater controls on public expression and movement put in place in its aftermath. The story focuses on the period 'after the disaster' rather than on the event of the earthquake itself, because Peace is 'interested in how we react to suffering, not the suffering itself. It is the battle that each of us takes with pain, defeat and suffering, [that] is what I want to understand.'[36] Consequently, his short story represents the aftermath of the earthquake through his protagonist's frustrated sense of injustice and experience of living under oppressive power and rule by fear imposed during this period. Covered in ash from the crumbling cityscape, Akutagawa and his neighbours resemble grey specters roaming across the ruins of their capital in shock and disbelief. When Akutagawa chances across his friend Yasunari, he almost fails to recognize him, exclaiming 'I was certain you must be dead! Sure you must be a ghost' (201). Yasunari simply replies 'Everyone is a ghost now […] or an orphan' (201). Propelled into a post-traumatic state, Peace's tale attempts to capture how the lives of those who survive the earthquake are changed forever.

The trauma of the earthquake and its aftershocks accentuates a compulsion to repeat. On a national level, it also inspires public terror and tightened government controls so intense that they force Akutagawa to reflect that '*It would have been better had we all died*' (202). Haunted by foreboding, and by repeated portents of doom including 'four crows' that land on four poles and caw four times (205), Akutagawa becomes distracted by images of 'Christ on the Cross' (202) and comes to view the earthquake as a punishment for humanity's sins. As a result, he chooses not to 'believe the official record. Ryūnosuke believed the earthquake had not stopped, would never stop. Ryūnosuke knew the disaster was still-to-come' (205). He becomes increasingly obsessed with the spectral presence of survivors among the ruins of the country and it's dead. These ghostly earthquake survivors haunt the altered landscape of Japan, and draw attention to the relationship between spectrality and oppression.

Consumed by guilt at the arbitrary nature of his own survival and by his exposure to death and suffering in the aftermath, Akutagawa is thrown into a near-constant state of anxiety that exacerbates his visual and auditory hallucinations. Plagued by déjà vu, his mental health declines rapidly following the earthquake, leading him to become trapped in a cyclical pattern of trauma and paranoia. Featuring a list of the many places burned or destroyed following the earthquake, Peace's narrative imports the spectral voices of news media and government information services to inject its narrative with rumours and counter-narratives regarding events and their consequences. Official updates are set against 'rumours of insurrection and invasion, their accusations of arson and looting, their whispers of rape and murder, their words of death and words of fear' (197). Akutagawa comprehends the earthquake as a logical extension of the mechanical grinding of his own mind, imagining 'turning gears and spinning cogwheels deep within the metallic body of the beast' (198). As time goes on, 'everywhere he saw gears and wheels, translucent against the earth, luminous against the sky, turning and spinning, grinding and screaming' (204). Extending the repeated image of cogs and wheels established by earlier stories in the cycle as a symbol of anxiety and psychological breakdown, these images are aligned in a post-traumatic society in which all is

> now withered, all now harrowed—
> *All now dead.* (200)

Both modernity and hauntology share a characteristic fracturing of experience, and of the self. Using hauntology as a critical practice to explore a deconstruction of the self, the city and the country as time out of joint, Peace conducts an invocation of the multiple contextual influences shaping cultural identity in Japan during the modernist period. Through the experiences of his protagonist Akutagawa, Peace offers an alternative narrative of modernism in Japan that puts heritage and history in dialogue with progress and change.

The ghosts of *Patient X* complicate the inheritance of the past, fracturing the present to reveal an alternative perspective on a modern Japan that 'is never gathered together, it is never at one with itself'.[37] As part of a wider exploration of tensions between modernity and history, the state and the self, Peace's tales repeatedly signal the agency of the return of the past in an increasingly controlled society in which the living and the dead coexist on a transitory plain. Amidst the apparent progress of the modernist period, the return of the past impedes the progress of the present, trapping Akutagawa in stasis. Through the intense singular experiences of this occupied character, Peace presents a fragmented sense of self as a meta-phor for the pressures enacted upon both the individual and the state by new Western influences and by the globalizing pressures of modernism in early twentieth century Japan.

SECOND SELF

Spectrality and time are closely connected in *Patient X*. Across the twelve short stories temporal boundaries begin to disintegrate, enabling the intrusion of the spectral into the realm of the everyday. The spectral double functions to highlight the unexpected nature of the return, rais-ing questions about the self and the Other, the individual and society. The frequent presence of mirrors and reflected imagery across the cycle underscores the displaced subjectivity and fragmented self of their shared protagonist Akutagawa. Making manifest the informing influences of Freud, Lacan, Poe and Dostoevsky through direct reference, as well as through symbolic allusion, Peace's twenty-first century short stories draw upon a literary heritage of doubling to offer new readings of the self and identity for a contemporary world. Peace argues that develop-ments in technology in the twenty-first century mean that 'our identities are increasingly divided. Today there is not a doppelgänger. There are endless [doppelgängers]. We live in a city where we are ghosts, in which no one knows anything about us.'[38] As a way of confronting this dual-ism in *Patient X*, his principal motif of the double offers a recurring reminder that Akutagawa is the specter that haunts the text in both theme and content. Dominated by the device of the double, the ghost writer and the ghost written, its individual stories combine to blur boundaries between recurrence and originality, life and death, past and present. The repetition of the same protagonist and subject across each of the stories in the collection does not function to reinforce a sense of identity, but instead conspires to undermine it, infusing each tale with a hermeneutic spectrality in a Kafka-esque fusion of gothic and historical narrative.

In the fifth short story, 'A Twice-Told Tale', protagonist Akutagawa openly discusses the works of 'Edgar Allan Poe' (84) with another writer friend in a café. Poe was one of America's earliest practitioners of the short story form, and is considered by some to be the inventor of detective fiction. Akutagawa's interest in Poe, and Poe's influence on his own short story practice, has been the subject of much critical and popular interest in Japan. Poe's work was translated in Japanese and attracted widespread praise from critics. Japanese novelist Soseki praised Poe for the 'mathematical structuring of his stories', 'laying out his design like a skilled engineer might' and even called him 'the founder of the short story'.[39] As an author, Akutagawa admired and attempted to emulate Poe's technique, and there is considerable evidence in his stories to suggest that Akutagawa had a pronounced understanding and appreciation of Poe's storytelling techniques. Peace also acknowledges the literary influence of Poe on his own work, claiming that 'Edgar Allan Poe is one of my favourite writers', and that in his short story collection *Patient X* 'the double story is my homage to him through Akutagawa'.[40]

In 'A Twice-Told Tale', Peace writes a homage to both Akutagawa and Poe by emulating their use of the double. The double, or 'doppelgänger' takes the form of a lookalike and has paranormal connotations as a harbinger of bad luck or doom. In German, the phrase literally translates as 'double walker' and, in literary representation, the character often bears a physical or behavioural resemblance as a counterpart to the self. The doppelgänger can harm its counterpart by putting bad thoughts into their mind, bringing them bad luck, inflicting illness, or acting as a portent of imminent death. Haunting the original as an unconscious dimension of their inner self, the appearance of the doppelgänger often gives rise to conflict. Functioning in manifold ways as an antagonist to the protagonist, the doppelgänger can operate as an external embodiment of a covert characteristic, signalling a separated form of the self that is made visible in the form of the Other. Throughout Peace's literary homage, protagonist Akutagawa is haunted by a doppelgänger who emerges from the shadows to physically stalk his day-to-day life.

In writing his short story, Peace drew on myths about psychological breakdowns, in which 'there was a doppelgänger and if you confronted them you were cursed'.[41] The epigraph for his story is taken from *Der Doppelgänger* ('The Double'), a song by Austrian composer Franz Schubert. This song is employed in the short story to punctuate narrative events, offering a sonic hauntology through lyrical refrain. The song tells the story of a singer who stands outside his old home and sees another man outside it, who is clearly in a state of 'torment'. He eventually reveals that the person he is watching is actually himself, the 'pale' image of a double that can 'ape' his own 'torment' of the past in the present. The use of this song as an epigraph raises key themes of imitation, doubling, space and time and psychological and emotional responses to replicas early in the story, establishing the tone and remit of the following tale.

Set in 'the Age of the Double' (84), 'A Twice-Told Tale' details an uncanny incident in which Akutagawa claims he is

> becoming trapped inside a tale by Poe. Just the other day, at an end of year party, I bumped into that one-legged German translator. He said he had seen me in a tobacco shop near here and was offended when I ignored him. But I was in Yokosuka at the time, teaching as usual. But when he described what had occurred, I realized this "second-self" of mine had been wearing exactly what I had been wearing that day: a raincoat. And this is the second time this has happened to me recently (84).

Akutagawa is inspired to wonder whether this double is 'a harbinger of luck? Even death?' (85), and across the short stories in the cycle sees his own image reflected back at him in fractured form through a series of mirrors and reflective surfaces that 'reflected him in endless doubles' (86). Each instance raises spectral associations with Lacan's mirror stage, offering a metaphorical statement on the divided self, representing the growing sense of paranoia experienced by the protagonist in his city environment. In a 'second-hand house of books, in your second-hand world of words', Akutagawa becomes haunted by the realization that his writing and his

> world of words, with its screens and its walls, with its windows and doors, is built from other people's books, other people's words, borrowed and bought, always, already stolen and used; in your second-hand house of books, in your second-hand world of words, your life is always, already second-hand, second-hand. (31)

As Akutagawa moves through the short story, he becomes haunted by acts of ghost writing that mirror his own literary endeavours. In a series of meetings with an old colleague, Jun'ichirō Tanizaki in a local café, he discovers that his friend is also planning to 'write something around the notion of doubles' (95). Tanizaki's repeated replies to his questions about this coincidence—'"Me, too," exclaimed the older man again. "How funny! Mine is almost finished and is the tale of two artists, Ōkawa and Aono. They are bitter rivals. But Ōkawa comes to see Aono as his doppelgänger and he even cites the famous story by Edgar Allan Poe"' (95). These haunting coincidences become so frequent that Akutagawa leaves the café feeling 'afraid' (96). On his way out, he realizes that his encounters with doubling are also being echoed in a sonic hauntology provided by the café's record-player. Feeling paranoid, Akutagawa checks the 'label on the record' and recognizes the connection—*'Schwanengesang – Schubert'* (96), a song about doubles. This is the final straw for Akutagawa, who turns to confront his friend, only to find 'his friend was not there. And at their table was only one coffee cup. His own coffee cup' (96).

Akutagawa attempts to finish the story he is trying to write, but he remains unsettled and easily distracted. In this state, he picks up 'a collection of stories by Edgar Allan Poe' (81) and settles on one story that is 'based on a brief article by Washington Irving [...] the protagonist was a young man who finds himself followed and thwarted at every turn by a masked figure' (81). This story, *William Wilson* (1839), details a confrontation between a protagonist and his double, in which the double is stabbed only to reveal that he is a mirror reflection of the killer, who has effectively committed suicide. In Washington Irving's source text for the story 'An Unwritten Drama of Lord Byron', a protagonist kills his double with a sword only to lift the double's mask and find his own face beneath it. The repetitive power of ghost writing is again explored later in Peace's short story, when Akutagawa browses through some books in a shop and selects the *'collected works of Dostoevsky'*, *'took down one volume, and you turned to its title page: the novella Dvoynik'* (97). This novel—*The Double*—tells the tale of a doppelgänger who takes over the life of a protagonist whose character and personality are the opposite of his own.

Even in his sleep, Akutagawa is haunted by a double that transgresses the realms of the real and the imaginary. In 'a garden which looked like the garden of his family home in Tabata' (82) he sees two children who 'seemed to be his children' (83) and enters his house to find 'a man in a Chinese-patterned yukata was lying on a futon on the floor. His eyes closed, a Holy Bible open on his chest, the man looked like Ryūnosuke; his exact double' (83). Repetition functions to create a dream-like quality and an uncanny lyrical dimension to the double images dreamt by Akutagawa. His reflections are hauntingly animated by the boy's final claim that 'you are still dreaming [...] It is your own reflection in the mirror' (84). Akutagawa gradually breaks down under the stress of these doubles, begins to sees multiple replicas of himself, and ends up in an asylum. Connecting mental illness to the society that produces these conditions, Peace's tale informs the representation of his protagonist's gradual decline into insanity across the text as a whole. Noting 'Goethe's title *Aus meinem Leben: Dichtung und Wahrheit*' (244), Akutagawa highlights an autobiography that relates the conditions of the times to the development of the individual. Suggesting that the contextual conditions of the period play an important role in the human psyche and condition, Peace's intertextual raising of Goethe functions to connect the socio-economic and political background of twentieth century Japan with the fractured identity of his protagonist subject.

Spectrality is predicated on an acknowledgment that the Other haunts the self. Throughout the interconnected short stories in *Patient X*, the double functions as an uncanny motif used by Peace to suggest an estrangement from the self though the form of an Other. Offering a paradoxical encounter with oneself, this narrative device makes visible internal divisions of the self through a rhetorical figure of contrast and repetition. The excessive sameness of this figure functions to subvert identification, epitomizing an internal struggle from which the self can escape only if it recognizes elements of its own shadow. Across *Patient X*, Peace deploys doubles as provocative metaphors that collectively challenge binary oppositions and the traumas of the past that disturb the present. Interactions between Akutagawa and his spectral doubles encourage readers to consider how and why the living interrogate their relationship to 'the dead' and to the past, exploring the fractured identities of the living, and the boundaries between the past and present. Through this exposure to Otherness in the form of the dislocated double, Peace's literary hauntology functions as a questioning of the self, and of the fragmented nature of contemporary society.

THE AFTERLIFE OF THE AUTHOR

As Chinese intellectual Li instructs Akutagawa in the seventh story of the collection 'After the War, Before the War—', during times of rapid change 'our immediate duty is to write' (157). In the stories that comprise the short story cycle *Patient X*, Peace mobilizes ghost-writing as a mode of spectral representation, a phantasmal form made possible through the agency offered by the act of the literary return. Mobilizing techniques of rewriting, repetition and doubling, his ghost-writing is spectral in both name and function, blurring boundaries between past and present versions of narratives, between Western and non-Western literatures, and occupying a ghostly space. As a result, his twenty-first century rewritings of early twentieth century Japanese short stories connect with and critique the many changes, traumas and conflicts of the contemporary moment. Exploring oppositions between the interior and exterior, the psyche and the social, East and West, his new short stories function as discrete units of representation as well as a coherent cycle of narratives that articulate a growing awareness of the dangers of dislocation from history. Confronting the beginnings of modernity, divisions in society and the fragmentation of the self, Peace uses rewriting to explore the fractured identities and haunted lives that characterize not only the early twentieth century Japan of Akutagawa's lifetime, but also the twenty-first century world of David Peace.

In *Patient X*, David Peace does not offer readers a conventional 'cherry blossom' vision of Japan. Critically engaging with concerns regarding Western influence and a widespread crisis of identity, Peace's rewritings instead intersect with wider trans-historical political, cultural, and economic discourses in the context of Japan at a historical turning point. His fictional Tokyo is a burnt-out shell of a city, suffering from the aftermath of natural disaster and the imposition of an ideological occupation. Engaging with this panorama, his short stories explore the personal and social effects of change, engaging with psychological responses to defeat through acts of destruction and creation. Rewriting narratives of the past to critique the 'ever-darkening times of naked self-interest and spiritual bankruptcy' (220) of twentieth century Japan, and of twenty-first century society, Peace attempts to solve not only 'the mystery of Akutagawa but the mystery of literature in general, to reveal the deep meaning'.[42]

Through the spectral dynamic of literature, Peace mobilizes hauntology to explain the present as well as the past. Locating and examining spectral presences within his text, he profiles a people and place haunted by contemporary anxieties about time, space and memory. Challenging the temporal stability of time, Peace gives voice to Akutagawa, invoking the ghost of the author and giving him agency in the present through the traumatic power of repetition and the occupation of his already established narratives. Revoicing, recycling and reviving Peace releases the spectral dynamic of the literary that suggests the agency of writing can illuminate not only the past, but also the present.

NOTES

1. Faber book jacket para-text in David Peace, *Patient X* [Proof Copy] (London: Faber, 2018).
2. *Patient X* is itself a reiteration of David Peace's 2016 short story collection *Fantasma* (meaning 'Ghost') published by Italian press Saggiatore. *Fantasma* contained five short stories and an essay that were originally written and published individually for a series of different occasions. As such, each story operated as a discrete narrative that was capable of standing singularly, but collectively they combined to offer a common protagonist to *Fantasma*, as well as connecting thematic concerns with the relationship between texts and rewrites, the individual and society, and the self and the Other. These themes and stories are extended, rewritten or augmented in *Patient X* to form a sequence of twelve short stories that chronicle the final years in the life of Ryūnosuke Akutagawa.
3. David Peace quoted by Poetarum Silva, 'FANTASMA, DI DAVID PEACE', *Poetarum Silva* <https://poetarumsilva.com/2016/04/12/fantasma-david-peace/>
4. David Peace, 'Radio Interview', *Radio Popolare*, March 2016 <http://www.radiopopolare.it/2016/03/david-peace-unanima-divisa-in-due/>
5. David Peace quoted in Annarita Briganti, 'Peace: "Preferisco le storie brevi il romanzo è minato dall'individualismo"', *La Repubblica.it*, 3 September 2016 <http://ricerca.repubblica.it/repubblica/archivio/repubblica/2016/03/09/peace-preferisco-le-storie-brevi-il-dallindividualismoMilano14.html>
6. Email from David Peace to Katy Shaw, 7.9.17.
7. Frank O'Connor, *The Lonely Voice: A Study of the Short Story* (Cleveland: World Publishing, 1963) p. 32.
8. David Peace quoted in Francesco Cancellato, 'David Peace: A volte ci cerchiamo su Google per scoprire chi siamo', *Linkiesta*, 12 March 2016 <http://www.linkiesta.it/it/article/2016/03/12/david-peace-a-volte-ci-cerchiamo-su-google-per-scoprire-chi-siamo/29570/>
9. David Peace, 'Radio Interview', *Fahrenheit.it*, 11 March 2016 <http://www.fahrenheit.rai.it/dl/portaleRadio/media/ContentItem-b57b62ff-b777-4254-a09d-0f7f652aab66.html#p=0>

10. G.H. Healey, 'Introduction', Ryūnosuke Akutagawa, *Kappa: A Novel* [1927] (trans.) Geoffrey Bownas (London: Peter Owen, 1970) p. 23.
11. Beongcheon Yu, *Akutagawa: An Introduction* (Detroit: Wayne State University Press, 1972) p. 21.
12. Howard Hibbet, 'Introduction', Ryūnosuke Akutagawa, *Rashomon and other Stories* (trans.) Takashi Kojima (Tokyo: Charles E Tuttle Company: 1952) p. 10.
13. David Peace quoted in Francesco Cancellato, 'David Peace: A volte ci cerchiamo su Google per scoprire chi siamo', *Linkiesta*, 12 March 2016 <http://www.linkiesta.it/it/article/2016/03/12/david-peace-a-volte-ci-cerchiamo-su-google-per-scoprire-chi-siamo/29570/>
14. Healey, 1970, p. 17.
15. Healey, 1970, p. 24.
16. Healey, 1970, p. 25.
17. Hibbet in Akutagawa, 1952, p. 9.
18. Healey, 1970, p. 43.
19. Healey, 1970, p. 41.
20. Haruki Murakami, 'Introduction', Ryūnosuke Akutagawa, *Rashomon and Other Stories* (trans.) Jay Rubin (London: Penguin, 2006) p. xxxi.
21. Healey, 1970, p. 29.
22. Healey, 1970, p. 13.
23. Healey, 1970, p. 17.
24. Roland Barthes, 'The Death of the Author', Eric Dayton (ed.) *Art and Interpretation: An Anthology of Readings in Aesthetics and the Philosophy of Art* (Peterborough, Ont.: Broadview, 1998) pp. 383–386; p. 386.
25. Originally written for a public lecture at the twelfth *Bridge The Gap?* Conference in Genoa, Italy organized by the Centre for Contemporary Art Kitakyushu, Japan in 2016.
26. The story of 'The Spider's Thread' was first recorded in writing as 'The Fable of the Onion', a story in which an evil woman is sent to hell because she has failed to do a good deed in her whole life. It is then noted that she had once given an onion to a beggar as an act of kindness. As a result, the angels use an onion to pull her from the pits of hell. But, as other sinners try to hang onto her clothes and join her escape, she kicks them off, and with this selfish act the onion breaks, sending her falling back into hell. The story was later rewritten by Dostoevsky as 'The Brothers Karamazov' (1917–18) and then by Akutagawa as 'The Spider's Thread'. Akutagawa's version of the story was first published in a children's magazine called *Akai Tori* (Red Bird) and draws on karmic teachings to offer a parable about selfless action. Based on a Buddhist parable published in Tokyo in 1895, the story describes the fate of Kandata, an evil robber who is damned to

hell before being offered a reprieve because he once saved the life of a spider. This spider is sent to help raise him out of hell on its thread, but the thread snaps when Kandata refuses to share it with other sinners who attempt to escape alongside him.

27. David Peace quoted in Francesco Cancellato, 'David Peace: A volte ci cerchiamo su Google per scoprire chi siamo', *Linkiesta*, 12 March 2016 <http://www.linkiesta.it/it/article/2016/03/12/david-peace-a-volte-ci-cerchiamo-su-google-per-scoprire-chi-siamo/29570/>

28. David Peace, 'Radio Interview', *Fahrenheit.it*, 11 March 2016 <http://www.fahrenheit.rai.it/dl/portaleRadio/media/ContentItem-b57b62ff-b777-4254-a09d-0f7f652aab66.html#p=0>

29. David Peace, 'Radio Interview', *Radio Popolare*, March 2016 <http://www.radiopopolare.it/2016/03/david-peace-unanima-divisa-in-due/>

30. David Peace quoted in Annarita Briganti, 'Peace: "Preferisco le storie brevi il romanzo è minato dall'individualismo"', *La Repubblica.it*, 3 September 2016 <http://ricerca.repubblica.it/repubblica/archivio/repubblica/2016/03/09/peace-preferisco-le-storie-brevi-il-dallindividualismoMilano14.html>

31. David Peace, 'David Peace Interviewed by Jorge: Podcast No. 144', *The Bat Segundo Show* <http://www.edrants.com/segundo/bss-144-david-peace/>

32. David Peace quoted in David Frati, 'Intervista a David Peace', *Mangialibri* <http://www.mangialibri.com/interviste/intervista-david-peace>

33. Derrida, 1994, p. 168.

34. Derrida, 1994, p. 125.

35. Derrida, 1994, p. 124.

36. David Peace quoted in Francesco Cancellato, 'David Peace: A volte ci cerchiamo su Google per scoprire chi siamo', *Linkiesta*, 12 March 2016 <http://www.linkiesta.it/it/article/2016/03/12/david-peace-a-volte-ci-cerchiamo-su-google-per-scoprire-chi-siamo/29570/>

37. Derrida, 1994, p. 16.

38. David Peace quoted in Francesco Cancellato, 'David Peace: A volte ci cerchiamo su Google per scoprire chi siamo', *Linkiesta*, 12 March 2016 <http://www.linkiesta.it/it/article/2016/03/12/david-peace-a-volte-ci-cerchiamo-su-google-per-scoprire-chi-siamo/29570/>

39. Lafeadio Hean, 'Poe's Verse', (ed.) John Erskine *Interpretations in Literature* (New York: Kennicat Press, 1965) p. 151.

40. David Peace, 'Radio Interview', *Fahrenheit.it*, 11 March 2016 <http://www.fahrenheit.rai.it/dl/portaleRadio/media/ContentItem-b57b62ff-b777-4254-a09d-0f7f652aab66.html#p=0>

41. David Peace, 'Radio Interview', *Fahrenheit.it*, 11 March 2016 <http://www.fahrenheit.rai.it/dl/portaleRadio/media/ContentItem-b57b62ff-b777-4254-a09d-0f7f652aab66.html#p=0>
42. David Peace quoted in David Frati, I'ntervista a David Peace', *Mangialibri* <http://www.mangialibri.com/interviste/intervista-david-peace>

Conclusion. 'In Return': Towards a Hauntology of Twenty-First Century English Literature

Abstract Using the power of literary representation to subvert and challenge, the twenty-first century authors profiled by this study stage various debates in relation to the specter, interrogating concepts of anxiety and justice, intertextuality and hospitality, selfhood and trauma. The conclusion reflects on why their works are most radical in their spectral moments and in their representation of a range of specters that refuse to submit to homogeneity, but rather disrupt and open up moments or issues to uncertainty, challenging both the writer and reader in the contemporary moment.

Keywords Hauntology • English literature • culture • past • present • Derrida • spectrality • contemporary • fiction • writings

In the twenty-first century 'the effort to live *with* ghosts [...] has superseded the traditional tendency to exorcise ghosts and lay them to rest'.[1] This contemporary fascination with specters and spectrality in English literature led Jeffrey Weinstock to reflect that 'our contemporary moment is a haunted one'.[2] Yet the 'increasing normalcy of the ghost'[3] as a subject of cultural representation in the contemporary period actually makes it harder for specters to be noticed. Blanco and Peeren's wry comment that 'ghosts are everywhere these days'[4] betrays a wider critical response to this hyper-visibility of ghosts in contemporary culture, a state which

© The Author(s) 2018
K. Shaw, *Hauntology*,
https://doi.org/10.1007/978-3-319-74968-6_6

paradoxically makes specters seem prominent and familiar, yet also harder to 'see' than ever before.

Derrida warned of this misleading presence/absence dynamic in his imagining of a time when 'one can no longer get any shut-eye, being so intent to watch out for the return'.[5] Made hyper-visible through the commercialization of ghosts as big business, and the popularity of haunting in tourist and heritage sites, contemporary culture undermines the unsettling effect of the specter by its incorporation into the aesthetic of the everyday.[6] An over-familiarity with the spectral in contemporary culture can desensitize the significance of their return and distract us from the relevance of the messages specters bring to the post-millennial world. As Andrew Smith warns, we tend to conceive of ghosts as 'historical beings because they are messengers about the preoccupations of a particular age' but in practice 'ghosts are never just ghosts; they provide us with an insight into what haunts our culture'.[7]

The spectral haunting of twenty-first century English culture encourages readers to revisit important ethical issues as well as historical and cultural heritages that remain unresolved in the present. Across the four case study texts explored by this Pivot, the intrusion of the spectral initiates a textual rupture, opening the text to the voice and knowledge of the spectral 'Other'. The ghost comes to signify the processes of being haunted—by the past, by other texts, and by those voices that have previously been marginalized or silenced. Speaking from this spectral position, the Other presents alternative or meta-critical perspectives that encourage a new awareness in both characters and readers.

In *Specters of Marx*, Derrida expresses hope that the new millennium will bear witness to the coming of 'another scholar',[8] one quite 'unlike his or her predecessor' who would be capable of 'thinking and of having commerce with the *revenants* and *arrivants* of history'.[9] Conscious of and responsive to the specters of the past in the present, such a scholar would be moved by a 'love' of 'justice [...]. The "scholar" of the future, the "intellectual" of tomorrow should learn it [...] from the ghost [...] by learning not how to make conversation with the ghost but how to talk with him, with her, how to let them speak or how to give them back speech.'[10] This appeal frames the concept of justice as a predicative necessity for both present knowledge and future progress, foregrounding the figurative possibility of the specter and the potential of that possibility as an unfulfilled promise. Positioning this investigation into and interaction with specters as more than simply a scholarly pursuit, Derrida argues that any such undertaking must be founded on, and inspired by, a profound belief in justice, a desire to look beneath and to search for alternatives to received histories, wisdoms and narratives of what has gone before. Any speaking about or to specters has to be conducted 'in the name of justice'.[11]

In their deconstructive capacity, specters posit this possibility of justice. The haunting return demands justice or, at the very least, a response from the haunted subject. Recognition of the specter is also recognition of the future inside the past, the possibilities opened up by new knowledge of that which went before. As the late, great, hauntology scholar Mark Fisher suggests, 'the long dark night at the end of history has to be grasped as an enormous opportunity [...]. From a situation in which nothing can happen, suddenly anything is possible again.'[12] Since specters return to offer an alternative to the present consensus, they also offer the scholar of the future opportunities and revisionary possibilities. Enabling a context in which 'anything is possible', their return does not signal the end of history but instead marks the advent of a new disjointed time in which past and present co-exist on a transitory plane. Invited or not, specters return in contemporary English literature, reactivating the presence of the past. In the realm of the literary, the living and the dead are free to speak and listen to one another. This dynamic enabled by the literary form is raised by Derrida's example of Shakespeare's *Hamlet* to suggest that justice can only be achieved in literary spectral interactions through the knowledge gained by dialogue with the specter that offers new understandings of both the self and the society. This task is not an easy one and, across the texts analysed in this Pivot, it is clear that the pursuit of spectral justice requires imagination, close reading and the rejection of received power and historical relations.

Using the power of literary representation to subvert and challenge, the twenty-first century authors profiled by this study also stage various debates in relation to the specter, interrogating concepts of anxiety and justice, intertextuality and hospitality, selfhood and trauma. Their works are most radical in their spectral moments and in their representations of a range of specters that refuse to submit to homogeneity. The radical agency of these specters lies in their ability to disrupt and open up moments or issues to uncertainty, challenging both writer and audience to recognize, engage or (re)consider.

Just as Derrida demands a reckoning with Marxism in *Specters of Marx*, so the new English literatures examined by this study demand a reckoning between contemporary readers and the past by recognizing and listening to the specters that haunt the present. Through their literary hauntologies, each text suggests that unless readers confront the immediate past, they will never be truly free to explore alternative futures and possibilities. In order to progress, protagonists must acknowledge the existence of such specters, and speak to and with them in order to access new insights and knowledge that can help inform the present moment and frame any future time. As part of this coming to terms with the specter, these texts are suggestive of the ways in which interactions between the self and the Other can enable new creative spaces for the acquisition of knowledge and the promotion of change. An extension of hospitality to ghosts invites a similar response from the reader, encouraging us to live with ghosts of the past in the present and to thereby become 'scholars of the future'.

As an intertextual concept, hauntology opens texts to other texts, as well as to the Other as a repressed or silenced element. Some of the analysed texts are haunted in a literal sense, in having a figure of a ghost as one of the characters appearing on the page or on the stage. Some texts are haunted through their presentation of the spectral perspective of the Other, the spectral space or the 'visor effect'. In each instance, haunting is conditional upon being noticed—recognition is a key source of agency for the specter and central to the success of the act of the return. In each text, the acceptance of the spectral without expectation is shown to enable a movement beyond the present into an alternative past, one that undermines the individual or collective psyche and, in doing so, illuminates alternatives that can offer new approaches and understandings for the future.

Framing haunting as a prerequisite for knowledge, these twenty-first century English literatures represent the possibilities and consequences that arise when contemporary characters offer hospitality to and recognize the specter out of the concern for justice that Derrida describes. The contemporary authors discussed in this study respond to Derrida's request and encourage readers to learn to live with ghosts and so become 'scholars of the future'. In each work, spectrality functions to highlight the need for justice, to illuminate the mistakes repeated across generations, and to present previously unknown inheritances or enact the remembering of something forgotten. When the specter emerges, it is not to passively reflect a present appetite for a golden-age of bygone pleasures, but rather because, as Gordon suggests, 'a repressed or unresolved social violence is making itself known [...]. These specters or ghosts appear when the trouble they represent and symptomize is no longer being contained or repressed or blocked from view'.[13] Foregrounding the social erasure of certain accounts of or experiences in the past, spectral agency encourages the haunted subject to acknowledge alternatives, 'blasting'—to use Benjamin's term[14]— the present by bringing to light the capacity for new narratives in the present. Making apparent the formerly inapparent, the return of the specter in the contemporary period politically repositions the marginalized and suggests that both are 'victims of the same condition and the same disappointed hope'.[15,16]

The interconnected nature of past, present and future is central to hauntology, a critical practice that is defined by conceptual interrelation. Hauntology is not possible without ontology, in much the same way as the dead cannot exist without the living. The return highlights the significance of identifying the impact of the past on the present, and the future. In landscapes saturated with memory and stained with history, protagonists ultimately find that, no matter how complicated the relations between past and present, they are inextricably connected; one is always necessary to define the other. Bringing critical focus to the influence of the past and the repetition of occurrences, hauntology emphasizes the pressing presence of the past in twenty-first century English literature. Representing a present occupied by the past, and preoccupied by the future, contemporary English literature deploys a variety of textual strategies to explore the role and function of specters in redefining the real. In the present moment that is a heterogeneous combination of past and future, specters signal unease at a perceived lack of progress from the past in the new millennium, and to the need for a future informed by the lessons of the past. Because in literature, when it comes to hauntology, the twenty-first century does not mark the end, but rather the end of the beginning.

NOTES

1. Blanco and Peeren, 2010, p. xiv.
2. Weinstock in Blanco and Peeren, 2013, p. 61.
3. Blanco and Peeren, 2010, p. xiv.
4. Blanco and Peeren, 2010, p. ix.
5. Derrida, 1994, p. 125.

6. Blanco and Peeren, 2010, pp. xiii–xiv. 'Ghosting' has itself become a key-word in the contemporary period. Also referred to as the 'slow fade' or 'the French exit', it accounts for the process whereby one party ceases all communication with the other in the hope that the other person will simply disappear, like a ghost. In this scenario, silence speaks louder than words, and a phantom-like fashion for withdrawing from communication and view attempts to redress the heightened visibility of the subject.

7. Andrew Smith, 'Hauntings', Catherine Spooner and Emma McEvoy (eds.) *The Routledge Companion to the Gothic* (London: Routledge: 2007) p. 153.

8. Derrida, 1994, p. 12.

9. Derrida, 1994, p. 176.

10. Derrida 1994, p. 76.

11. Derrida, 1994, p. xviii.

12. Fisher, 2009. p. 81.

13. Gordon, 2008, p. xvi.

14. Walter Benjamin suggests that the critical momentum of historical materialism 'is registered in that blasting of historical continuity' that liquidates the continuum of history, and in doing so 'blasts out "the reified" continuity of history' (Walter Benjamin, *On the Concept of History, in Selected Writings: Volume Four* Howard Eiland (ed.) and Michael W. Jennings (trans.) Edmund Jephcott (Cambridge: Harvard University Press, 2003) p. 26.

15. Horkheimer and Adorno, 2002, p. 215.

16. Jameson in Sprinker, 2008, p. 40.

BIBLIOGRAPHY

Akutagawa, Ryūnosuke. *Kappa: A Novel* [1927] (trans.) Geoffrey Bownas (London: Peter Owen, 1970)

Akutagawa, Ryūnosuke. *Rashomon and Other Stories* (trans.) Jay Rubin (London: Penguin, 2006)

Akutagawa, Ryūnosuke. *Rashomon and Other Stories* (trans.) Takashi Kojima (Tokyo: Charles E Tuttle Company, 1952)

Armitage, Simon. *Killing Time* (London: Faber and Faber, 1999)

Baudrillard, Jean. *The Illusion of the End* (trans.) Chris Turner (Stanford: Stanford University Press, 1994)

Benjamin, Walter. *On the Concept of History, in Selected Writings: Volume Four,* Eiland, Howard and Jennings (eds.), Michael W. (trans.) Edmund Jephcott (Cambridge: Harvard University Press, 2003)

Billington, Michael. 'Great Performances' *The Guardian*, 13 April 2015 <https://www.theguardian.com/stage/2015/apr/13/theatre-great-performances-actor-mark-rylance-jerusalem-2009>

Blanco, Maria del Pilar and Peeren, Esther (eds.), *Popular Ghosts: The Haunted Spaces of Everyday Culture* (London: Continuum, 2010)

Blanco, Maria del Pilar and Peeren, Esther (eds.) *The Spectralities Reader* (London: Bloomsbury, 2013)

Bollen, Christopher. "Interview: Zadie Smith', *Interview Magazine* <http://www.interviewmagazine.com/culture/zadie-smith/print/>

Bragg, Billy. *The Progressive Patriot* (London: Black Swan, 2007)

© The Author(s) 2018
K. Shaw, *Hauntology*,
https://doi.org/10.1007/978-3-319-74968-6

Bridle, James. 'Hauntological Futures', *booktwo.org*, 20 March 2011 <http://booktwo.org/notebook/hauntological-futures/>

Briganti, Annarita. 'Peace: "Preferisco le storie brevi il romanzo è minato dall'individualismo"', *La Repubblica.it*, 3 September 2016 <http://ricerca.repubblica.it/repubblica/archivio/repubblica/2016/03/09/peace-preferisco-le-storie-brevi-il-dallindividualismoMilano14.html>

Brooks, Peter. *The Empty Space* (Harmondsworth: Penguin, 1968)

Buse, P and Stott, A (eds.). *Ghosts: Deconstruction, Psychoanalysis, History* (London: Palgrave, 1999)

Butterworth, Jez. 'Theater Talk: "Jerusalem" Playwright Jez Butterworth and Tony-winning Best Actor, Mark Rylance', *CunyTV75: Youtube* <https://www.youtube.com/watch?v=ENEoRHLuZlI>

Butterworth, Jez. *Jerusalem* (London: Nick Hern Books, 2009)

Butterworth, Jez. *Mojo and a Filmmaker's Diary* (London: Faber, 1998)

Cancellato, Francesco. 'David Peace: A volte ci cerchiamo su Google per scoprire chi siamo', *Linkiesta*, 12 March 2016 <http://www.linkiesta.it/it/article/2016/03/12/david-peace-a-volte-ci-cerchiamo-su-google-per-scoprire-chi-siamo/29570/>

Caputo, J.D. *Deconstruction in a Nutshell: A Conversation with Jacques Derrida* (New York: Fordham University Press, 2002)

Castricano, Jodey. *Cryptomimesis: The Gothic and Jacques Derrida's Ghost Writing* (London: McGill-Queens University Press, 2001)

Chesterton, G.K. *Charles Dickens: A Critical Study* (New York: Dood Mead and Company, 1906)

Cixous, Hélène. 'When the Word Is a Stage', *New Literary History*, Vol. 37 No 1 (Winter 2006) pp. 107–117.

Cixous, Hélène. *Three Steps on the Ladder of Writing* (New York: Columbia University Press, 1994)

Coughlan, David. *Ghost Writing in Contemporary American Fiction* (London: Palgrave, 2016)

Dalrymple, Theodore. 'Zadie Smith's London', *City Journal*, Winter 2013 <http://www.city-journal.org/html/zadie-smith%E2%80%99s-london-13541.html>

Dayton, Eric (ed.). *Art and Interpretation: An Anthology of Readings in Aesthetics and the Philosophy of Art* (Peterborough: Broadview, 1998)

De Certeau, Michael. *The Practice of Everyday Life* (trans.) Steven Rendall (Berkley, LA: University of California Press, 1984)

DeLilo, Don. *Mao II* (New York: Viking, 1991)

Derrida, Jacques. 'Force of Law: The "Mystical Foundation of Authority"', in: *Deconstruction and the Possibility of Justice*, Drucilla Cornell, Michel Rosenfeld and David Gray Carlson (eds). (London: Routledge, 1992)

Derrida, Jacques. 'The Ghost Dance: An Interview with Jacques Derrida', *Public*, 2, 1989, pp.60–73.

Derrida, Jacques. *Adieu to Emmanuel Levinas* (trans.) Michael Naas (London: Standford University Press, 1999)

Derrida, Jacques. *Memories: For Paul de Man* (New York: Columbia University Press, 1986)

Derrida, Jacques. *Of Hospitality: Anne Dufourmantelle Invites Jacques Derrida to Respond* (Stanford: Stanford University Press, 2000)

Derrida, Jacques. *Specters of Marx: The State of the Debt, the Work of Mourning and the New International* (trans.) Peggy Kamuf (London: Routledge, 1994)

Derrida, Jacques. *The Ear of the Other: Otobiography, Transference, Translation: Texts and Discussions with Jacques Derrida* (trans.) Peggy Kamuf (Nebraska: University of Nebraska Press, 1988)

Derrida, Jacques. *The Gift of Death & Literature in Secret (Religion and Postmodernism)* (Chicago: Chicago University Press, 2008)

Douglas, Mary. *Mary Douglas Collected Works Volume II: Purity and Danger: An Analysis of Concepts of Pollution and Taboo* (London: Routledge, 2003)

Dubreuil, Laurent. 'The Presences of Deconstruction', *New Literary History*, Vol. 37 No. 1.

Edemariam, Aida. 'The Saturday Interview: Jez Butterworth', *The Guardian*, 14 May 2011 <https://www.theguardian.com/theguardian/2011/may/14/saturday-interview-jez-butterworth>

Erskine, John (ed.). *Interpretations in Literature* (New York: Kennicat Press, 1965)

Fisher, Mark. 'Phonograph Blues', *K-Punk: Abstract Dynamics*, 19 October 2006 <http://k-punk.abstractdynamics.org/archives/008535.html>

Fisher, Mark. 'Specters of Accelerationism', *K-Punk: Abstract Dynamics*, 28 October 2008 <http://k-punk.abstractdynamics.org/archives/010782.html>

Fisher, Mark. *Capitalist Realism* (Winchester: Zero Books, 2009)

Fisher, Mark. *Ghosts of My Life* (Winchester: Zero Books, 2014)

Frank, Jason A and Tamborino, John. *Vocations of Political Theory* (Minneapolis: University of Minnesota Press, 2000)

Frati, David. 'Intervista a David Peace', *Mangialibri* <http://www.mangialibri.com/interviste/intervista-david-peace>

Freud, Sigmund. *The Standard Edition of the Complete Psychological Works of Sigmund Freud* (trans.) James Strachey and Anna Freud (London: Hogarth, 1986)

Gordon, Avery. *Ghostly Matters: Haunting and the Sociological Imagination* (Minneapolis: University of Minnesota Press, 2008)

Harpin, Anna. 'Land of Hope and Glory: Jez Butterworth's Tragic Landscapes', *Studies in Theatre and Performance*, Vol. 31, No 1 (2011) pp. 61–73.

Harris, Verne. 'Hauntology, Archivy and Banditry: An Engagement with Derrida and Zapiro', *Critical Arts*, Vol. 29, No 1 (2015) pp.13–27.

Hemming, Sarah. 'Jez Butterworth's Play Hits the West End', *Financial Times*, 29 January 2010 <http://www.ft.com/cms/s/0/03f4c2da-0c64-11df-a941-00144feabdc0.html>

Holdsworth, Natalie and Luckhurst, Mary (eds.). *A Concise Companion to Contemporary British and Irish Drama* (Chichester: Wiley Blackwell, 2013)

Horkheimer, Max and Adorno, Theodor W. (eds.) *The Dialectic of Enlightenment: Philosophical Fragments* (trans.) Edmund Jephcott (Stanford: Stanford University Press, 2002)

Janda, Laura A. 'The Conceptualization of Events and their Relationship to Time in Russian', *Glossos*, Issue 2, Winter 2002.

Kermode, Frank. *The Sense of an Ending: Studies in the Theory of Fiction* (New York: OUP, 1967)

Kronick, Jospeh G. *Derrida and the Future of Literature* (New York: Suny Press, 1999)

Laclau, Ernesto. 'The Time Is Out of Joint', *Diacritics*, Vol. 25, No. 2 (Summer 1995) pp. 85–96.

Loevlie, Elisabeth M. 'Faith in the Ghosts of Literature: Poetic Hauntology in Derrida, Blanchot and Morrison's Beloved', *Religions* 2013, 4, pp. 336–350.

Luckhurst, Mary and Morin, Emilie (eds.). *Theatre and Ghosts: Materiality, Performance and Modernity* (London: Palgrave, 2014)

Lyotard, Jean-Francois. *Postmodern Condition: A Report on Knowledge (Theory & History of Literature)* (Manchester: Manchester University Press, 1984)

Macdonald, Alex. 'Jaundiced Reality: Simon Armitage Interviewed', *The Quietus*, 12 October 2014 <http://thequietus.com/articles/16464-simon-armitage-paper-aeroplanes-interview-next-generation-poetry>

Mangan, Michael. *Staging Masculinities* (Basingstoke: Palgrave, 2003)

Marr, Andrew. 'Evictions, Protests, Unrest: How Jerusalem Saw them Coming', *BBC News*, 24 October 2011 <http://www.bbc.co.uk/news/magazine-15427879>

McBee, Thomas Page. 'The Rumpus Interview with Zadie Smith', *The Rumpus*, 1 January 2013 <http://therumpus.net/2013/01/the-rumpus-interview-with-zadie-smith/>

Miller, Laura. '"NW": Zadie Smith's Neighborhood', *Salon*, 27 August 2012 <http://www.salon.com/2012/08/26/nw_zadie_smiths_neighborhood/>

Motion, Andrew. '2000: Zero Gravity: The Millennium Report', *The Guardian*, 27 December 1999 <https://www.theguardian.com/books/1999/dec/27/poetry.millennium>

Murray, Alex. 'Hauntology; Or, Capitalism Is Dead, Let's Eat It's Corpse!', MA Thesis (Manchester: Manchester Metropolitan University, 2015)

Nasta, Susheila (ed.). *Writing across Worlds: Contemporary Writers Talk* (London: Routledge, 2004)

Natoli, Joseph and Hutcheon, Linda (eds.). *A Postmodern Reader* (New York: State University Press of New York, 1993)

Nield, Sophie. 'Theatre of Screams: On Ghosts and Drama', *The Guardian*, 1 Nov 2010 <https://www.theguardian.com/stage/theatreblog/2010/nov/01/theatre-ghost-drama>

O'Brien, Eugene. 'Guests of a Nation: Geists of a Nation', *New Hibernia Review*, Vol. 11, No. 3 (Autumn 2007) pp. 114–130.

O'Brien, Eugene. '"More than a Language…No More of a Language": Merriman, Heaney, and the Metamorphoses of Translation', *Irish University Review*, Vol. 34 No. 2 (Autumn-Winter 2004) pp. 277–290.

O'Connor, Frank. *The Lonely Voice: A Study of the Short Story* (Cleveland: World Publishing, 1963)

O'Gorman, Kevin D. 'Modern Hospitality: Lessons from the Past', *Journal of Hospitality and Tourism Management* 12 (2) 2005, pp. 141–151.

Olick, Jeffrey K., Vinitzky, Vered and Daniel Levy (eds.) *The Collective Memory Reader* (Oxford: Oxford University Press, 2011)

Peace, David. 'David Peace Interviewed by Jorge: Podcast No. 144', *The Bat Segundo Show* <http://www.edrants.com/segundo/bss-144-david-peace/>

Peace, David. 'Radio Interview', *Fahrenheit.it*, 11 March 2016a <http://www.fahrenheit.rai.it/dl/portaleRadio/media/ContentItem-b57b62ff-b777-4254-a09d-0f7f652aab66.html#p=0>

Peace, David. 'Radio Interview', *Radio Popolare*, March 2016b <http://www.radiopopolare.it/2016/03/david-peace-unanima-divisa-in-due/>

Peace, David. *Patient X* (London: Faber, 2018)

Peeren, Esther. *The Spectral Metaphor: Living Ghosts and the Agency of Invisibility* (London: Palgrave Macmillan, 2014)

Poetarum Silva, 'FANTASMA, DI DAVID PEACE', *Poetarum Silva* <https://poetarumsilva.com/2016/04/12/fantasma-david-peace/>

Potts, Robert. 'Mean Time', *The Guardian*, 15 December 1999 <https://www.theguardian.com/books/1999/dec/15/poetry.artsfeatures>

Raphael, Timothy. 'Mo(u)rning in America: Hamlet, Reagan, and the Rights of Memory', *Theatre Journal*, Vol. 59, No. 1 (March 2007) pp. 1–20.

Reynolds, Simon. *Retromania: Pop Culture's Addiction to its Own Past* (London: Faber, 2012)

Roberts, Michael Simmons and Farley, Paul. *Edgelands: Journeys into England's True Wilderness* (London: Vintage, 2012)

Rosello, Mireille. *Postcolonial Hospitality: The Immigrant as Guest* (Stanford: Stanford University Press, 2001)

Schor, Esther. *Bearing the Dead: The British Culture of Mourning from the Enlightenment to Victoria* (London: Princeton University Press, 1994)

Self, John. 'Zadie Smith Interview', *Asylum* <https://theasylum.wordpress.com/2012/09/12/zadie-smith-interview/>

Sim, Stuart. *Postmodern Encounters: Derrida and the End of History* (Cambridge: Icon Books UK, 1999)

Smith, Zadie. 'Dead Man Laughing', *The New Yorker*, 22 December 2008 <http://www.newyorker.com/magazine/2008/12/22/dead-man-laughing>

Smith, Zadie. *Changing my Mind Essays* (London: Penguin, 2009)

Smith, Zadie. *NW* (London: Penguin, 2012)

Spooner, Catherine and McEvoy, Emma (eds.). *The Routledge Companion to the Gothic* (London: Routledge: 2007)

Sprinker, Michael (ed.). *Ghostly Demarcations: A Symposium on Jacques Derrida's Specters of Marx* (London: Verso, 2008)

Strozier, Charles B. *The Year 2000: Essays on the End* (London: New York University Press, 1997)

Weaver, David (ed.). *The American Journalist in the 21st Century: U.S. News People at the Dawn of a New Millennium* (New York: Routledge, 2006)

Weinstock, Jeffrey (ed.). *Spectral America: Phantoms and the National Imagination* (London: University of Wisconsin Press, 2004)

Wolfreys, Julian. *Victorian Hauntings: Spectraloty, Gothic, the Uncanny and Literature* (London: Palgrave, 2001)

Yu, Beongcheon. *Akutagawa: An Introduction* (Detroit: Wayne State University Press, 1972)

Žižek, Slavoj. *Looking Awry: An Introduction to Jacques Lacan through Popular Culture* (London: The MIT Press, 1992)

Index[1]

A

Absence, 1, 6, 7, 19, 30, 31, 33, 48, 50, 51, 70, 106

Armitage, Simon, 17, 25–42

B

Butterworth, Jez, 17, 23n104, 43–58

C

Contemporary, 3, 4, 8, 12–19, 20n12, 25, 26, 29–34, 36, 39, 43–46, 48, 49, 51, 54–56, 60, 61, 64–69, 71, 75, 77, 78, 85–88, 94, 98, 99, 101n25, 105–109, 110n6

D

Derrida, Jacques, 2, 4–12, 15, 16, 18, 19n1, 20n8, 20n11, 20n12, 20n15, 20n16, 20n18, 20n19, 20n21–26, 21n29–31, 21n33–36, 21n40, 21n41, 21n43, 21n45, 21n48, 21n51, 21n53, 21n55, 21n56, 21n58, 21n60–63, 22n65–67, 22n81, 23n94, 23n95, 23n97, 23n98, 23n100, 42n22, 42n23, 42n29, 60–63, 78, 79n5, 79n7, 79n9, 79n10–25, 80n33–36, 81n45, 81n47, 91, 102n33–35, 102n37, 106–108, 109n5, 110n8–11

Double, 18, 35, 51, 52, 60, 71–78, 84, 88, 94–98

Drama, 3, 17, 36, 44–48, 51, 54–56, 58n24, 70

E

England, 2, 13, 18, 26, 27, 29, 30, 35, 36, 41n10, 44–46, 48, 51, 53, 55, 56, 56n1, 58n24, 60, 61, 65–67, 77, 78, 84

[1] Note: Page numbers followed by 'n' refer to notes.

© The Author(s) 2018
K. Shaw, *Hauntology*,
https://doi.org/10.1007/978-3-319-74968-6

F

Future, 2, 3, 5, 7, 8, 10–15, 18, 19, 20n12, 26, 27, 29–31, 37–40, 44, 54, 55, 60, 67, 71, 72, 87, 106–109

G

Ghost, 1–23, 27, 29, 38, 43, 44, 46, 48, 54–56, 63, 77, 84, 86–88, 90–94, 96, 97, 99, 100n2, 105, 106, 108, 109, 110n6

Guest, 60–64, 68, 69, 71, 74, 76

H

Haunting, 2, 3, 6, 7, 9, 11–13, 15–18, 20n12, 29, 32, 34, 35, 37, 38, 44, 45, 48, 49, 55, 56, 76, 83, 84, 86, 87, 91, 95, 97, 106–108, 110n7

Hauntology, 1–23, 63, 84, 91, 93, 95, 97–99, 105–110

Home, 18, 35, 49, 51–53, 61–65, 68–72, 74–76, 78, 81n46, 95, 97

Hospitality, 9, 10, 18, 53, 60–65, 68–71, 75, 77–79, 81n46, 107, 108

I

Intertextual, 15–17, 44–46, 48–50, 54–56, 58n24, 88, 98, 108

L

London, 18, 27, 35, 40n7, 41n10, 46, 57n2, 58n24, 64–68, 72, 76, 77

M

Media, 4, 13, 25, 28, 31–34, 36–38, 40, 41n16, 93

Millennial, 17, 25–30, 32, 34, 35, 37, 39, 40

N

Novel, 3, 18, 58n24, 59–61, 64–68, 70, 71, 73, 77–79, 84, 85, 97

O

Other, 7, 10, 11, 18, 19, 51, 54, 60, 62–64, 68–71, 76, 78, 81n46, 87, 90, 94–96, 98, 100n2, 106, 108, 109

P

Past, 2–19, 20n12, 25–27, 29–31, 37–39, 41n10, 44–47, 49, 50, 52, 55, 56, 56n2, 60, 61, 65, 67, 71, 77, 78, 87, 89–91, 93, 94, 96, 98–100, 106–109

Peace, David, 18, 23n108, 83–103

Poetry, 3, 27, 28, 34, 40, 58n24

Post-millennial, 3, 14, 19, 44, 56, 58n24, 60, 84, 106

Power, 4, 10, 14, 15, 29, 34, 39, 44, 46, 51–55, 60–64, 67–69, 71, 73, 74, 92, 97, 100, 107

R

Rewriting, 17, 83, 84, 87–91, 99

Ryūnosuke Akutagawa, 83–85, 88, 89, 92, 97, 100n2, 101n10, 101n12, 101n20

S

Self, 2, 11, 18, 19, 28, 44, 45, 49, 52, 59–81, 87, 89, 90, 93–99, 100n2, 107, 108

Short story, 3, 18, 19, 83, 85–88, 90–92, 94–99, 100n2

Smith, Zadie, 18, 23n107, 59–81

Society, 5, 7, 11–13, 19, 25, 27, 33, 34, 36, 37, 39, 43–46, 48, 49, 51, 53, 55, 60, 66, 67, 75, 78, 84–86, 90, 91, 93, 94, 98, 99, 100n2, 107

Space, 2, 3, 6–10, 14, 16–19, 30, 32, 45, 46, 48, 49, 51, 53, 54, 56, 60–63, 65–72, 77, 78, 84, 87, 90, 91, 96, 99, 108

Spectral, 2–19, 20n12, 25–47, 50–52, 54–56, 60, 61, 64, 65, 70, 76–78, 84, 90–94, 96, 98–100, 105–109

Specters of Marx, 4–7, 9, 11, 18, 106, 108

Stage, 10, 17, 43–45, 48, 50–54, 57n2, 58n24, 69, 96, 107–109

T

Time, 2, 4, 6–9, 11, 12, 15–19, 20n12, 26, 28–31, 34, 35, 37–40, 40n2, 41n10, 44, 45, 47, 49–53, 55, 65, 67–75, 77, 78, 84–86, 91–94, 96, 98, 99, 106–108

U

Uncanny, 15, 17, 18, 43, 48, 49, 52, 56, 60, 61, 67, 69, 71, 77, 84, 96–98

Unconditional, 10, 15, 18, 61–64, 71, 78, 79

CPSIA information can be obtained
at www.ICGtesting.com
Printed in the USA
LVHW03*0026310718
585364LV00007B/273/P

9 783319 749679